# The Leader Who Is Hardly Known:

## Self-less Teaching from the Chinese Tradition

Steven Simpson, Ph.D.

Published by:

Wood 'N' Barnes Publishing & Distribution
Oklahoma City, Oklahoma 73112
405-942-6812

Chapter 10, "The Inventor's Mantle Clock" appeared in a slightly different form under the title "In Nature We See Ourselves: A Lesson from the Tao" in *Call to Earth: Journal of the International Association for Environmental Philosophy*, 2001, Vol.II, No. 2, pp. 12-15. Chapter 11, "The Interrupted Stargazers" appeared in a slightly different form under the title "A Simple Lesson in Experiencing Nature," in *The Journal of Experiential Education*, 1999, Vol. 22, No. 3, pp.118-122.

Calligraphy by Hsieh Shih
Cover Design by Blue Designs
Copyediting & Design by Ramona Cunningham

Printed in the United States of America
Oklahoma City, Oklahoma
ISBN # 1-885473-51-6

To Manyu and Clare

The Chinese calligraphy in this book was done by Hsieh Shih.
He was a career soldier with the
Nationalist Army of the Republic of China.
Now in his late seventies, Mr. Hsieh is retired
and practices his art in Taipei.

# Acknowledgements

Many people helped me with this book. Wang Shin of National Taiwan University and Lan Hai-xia of the University of Wisconsin-La Crosse offered guidance on Taoist philosophy. Buzz Bocher and Dan Miller of the Institute for Experiential Education were my experts on experiential education. Buzz and Dan, along with Pat O'Hara, Stefan Smith, Jen Stanchfield, Christy Marek, Nancy Navar, George Arimond, and Amanda Deschene reviewed the manuscript and made excellent suggestions for improving it. Ed Grant and Nancy Stuart provided many experiences that ended up as stories in the book. Kelly Cain, Dan Creely, Tsai Huei-min, Nora Lan-hung Chiang, and Leo McAvoy showed me elements of the Leader Who is Hardly Known in their teaching.

Manyu Hsieh Simpson, my wife, also offered guidance concerning the Tao. Her help, however, came more from her lifestyle than her academic training in Tao philosophy. When we first met in Taiwan, I wrote about her to friends in the United States. At the time her English was not very good, so when she learned that I described her as "simple" in my letters, she was offended. Now she realizes that it was one of the biggest compliments that I could have given and probably was the inspiration for this book. The writing of this book coincides almost exactly with the first four years of my daughter Clare's life. There is no telling how much of her is in these pages.

A special thank you to my father-in-law, Hsieh Shih, whose Chinese calligraphy helped to convey a reflective tone for the book.

The University of Wisconsin-La Crosse provided me with both a one-year sabbatical and a faculty research grant. Without this support, the book would not have been written.

Finally I want to thank David Wood and Mony Cunningham at Wood N' Barnes Publishing. They let me write the book that I wanted to write, then worked with me to make it better.

# Contents

道　Introduction

This book is a commentary on the many commonalities and the oc-
casional differences between Tao philosophy and experiential education theory and practice. While the general idea for the book came
slowly as I encountered passage after passage from Tao literature
that had direct application to my work as an experiential educator,
the spark that moved me to sit down and start writing was a single
verse from the Tao classic, *Tao Te Ching*. Considered the cornerstone of Taoist philosophy, the *Tao Te Ching* was written about 2,500
years ago and is attributed to Lao-tzu, "the Old Master." The ancient
book consists of eighty-one short chapters of poetic prose and is a
primer on individual well-being, social harmony, leadership, and
humanity's relationship with nature. Even those who have never
read the *Tao Te Ching* will be familiar with some of its lessons. Its
most famous quote, for example, is "A journey of a thousand miles
begins with a single step."[1]

The verse that spurred me to write a book about Tao thinking and
experiential education, however, is not the one about the thousand-mile journey. Instead it was a passage from Chapter 17, and
the subject was leadership. An excerpt from that chapter reads:

> *True leaders are hardly known to their followers...*
> *When the work's done right,*
> *With no fuss or boasting,*
> *Ordinary people say,*
> *Oh, we did it.*[2]

At first glance, the quotation does not seem to deserve an entire
book. All it says is that when exceptional leaders do their best
work, it is others who are instilled with a sense of accomplish-

ment. This sentiment is common knowledge to most experiential educators; it is appealing but does not seem especially profound. Looked at carefully, however, the passage offers insights into one of the basic issues of experiential education, something I call the experiential educator's dilemma.

## LEADERS AND FACILITATORS

The experiential educator's dilemma is the conflicting goals of an educator wanting to influence students in specific ways, yet simultaneously wanting those students to take responsibility for their own learning. Put another way, it is the constant attempt to balance instructor guidance with student freedom and independence. All education programs need vision, goals, information, and creative thinking. The dilemma is knowing how much of these things should come from the teacher and how much from the students.

Finding the balance between teacher-driven education and student-driven education, of course, is not easy. There is no single correct position. It is like the rolla-bolla, the plank and cylinder apparatus that circus jugglers sometimes stand on during their performances. The center of balance shifts continuously and is very seldom dead center. Yet while maintaining the proper balance is difficult, it is basic to success.

Even the jargon of experiential education recognizes the experiential educator's dilemma. The terms "leader" and "facilitator," two of the most common names for people who work in experiential education, are good examples. While the terms are sometimes used interchangeably, the distinction between the two is really the difference between education with the teacher making the decisions and education with the students in that role. Being a "leader," at least in the traditional use of the word, suggests having a vision and moving people to action toward a specific end. Leaders possess knowledge that other people in the group do not have, and either by respect or by granted authority, leaders use that knowledge to guide people in specific directions and get them to accomplish tasks they would not have achieved on their own.

"Facilitators," on the other hand, do not so much provide vision as afford opportunity. Facilitation, unlike leadership, asks students to establish their own goals, identify their own problems, and know what it is they want to learn. The facilitator's job is to help students discover their own educational goals and then to provide experiences that address those goals. On a ropes and challenge course, for example (where the term facilitator is commonplace), the facilitator first learns if a group of participants wants to work on self-esteem, conflict resolution, teamwork, etc..., then develops a series of initiatives and activities that addresses that group's self-determined goals and objectives.

The point to be made here is not to argue semantics, but to identify a real conflict in the basic goals of experiential education. From a leadership perspective, a teacher who has wisdom and vision should readily share them. By getting students to adopt a shared vision or understand new information, the teacher's vision and guidance lead students to an educational foundation and a solid body of knowledge. Conversely, from a facilitation perspective, an educator does not impose his or her vision on the participants. The individual facilitator cannot even be sure that his or her knowledge is actually what a particular group of students needs. There is always an under-riding sense that self-discovery may be a better instructor than any teacher-directed program. Allowing students to determine their own direction and explore their own interests can be slow and initially chaotic, but it breeds a philosophy of experiencing. Instilling such a philosophy may, in the long run, be a better leadership objective than whatever the educator thinks is needed at that specific moment.

From a Tao perspective, the experiential educator's dilemma would be seen as an example of complementary opposites. And as complementary opposites, the solution to the dilemma is not all one extreme and none of the other. An educator is not just a leader or just a facilitator, but is a leader-facilitator. As a leader, he or she must set a direction for students that is consistent with Tao tenets. The direction, however, has many paths (the Tao is not, after all, indoctrination or coercion), so as facilitator the educator must guarantee that students have the freedom and flexibility to find the path that is best for them. Then, as Chapter 17 of the *Tao Te Ching* reminds us, this should be done with such subtlety that the students feel as though the educator was hardly involved.

Sometimes those in experiential education feel that in order for students to feel a strong personal sense of accomplishment, the students have to be in the primary decision-making role. This assumption actually is not correct. Perhaps the long-range goal of experiential education is to teach students the skills to eventually assume full responsibility for their education, but until those skills are learned, experiential education is student-centered rather than student-directed.[3] The sense of accomplishment is a perception, and as a perception, it occurs even when a leader determines the direction of the program and chooses most of the tasks. There is a difference between being independent and feeling a sense of personal accomplishment. A ropes course facilitator, for example, after helping a group establish their goals, will choose the activities for the group and set up the high elements. He or she, in fact, may do everything for the students except the actual climbing. Still when one of those students is asked to describe how it felt to hook into the belay system, climb a pole thirty feet into the air, and throw himself into space, the answer will almost certainly be, "I can't believe I did that on my own!" And this is only one example. The same applies when a student completes her first night hike, advances to a yellow belt in tae kwon do, or hits her first home run.

In each of these examples, the students would be correct in thinking that they accomplished something on their own. This is especially true if the leader, while laying all the groundwork, had consciously remained in the background. Teacher guidance and significant student accomplishment are not mutually exclusive. Kenneth Boulding expressed this sentiment well when he wrote:

> As every good teacher knows, the business of teaching is...
> that of co-operating with the student's own inward teacher
> whereby the student's image may grow in conformity with
> that of his outward teacher.[4]

Being a Leader Who is Hardly Known, of course, puts high demands on experiential educators. To be a guiding force, yet remain hardly noticed, requires a teaching master, a Socrates in both range of knowledge and teaching skill. Such a teacher cannot get away with merely providing students with basic skills, then turning them loose. Instead the teacher's knowledge must be broad enough to work effectively with students who may take alternative routes toward a common end. That knowledge must also be deep enough to move with students as they take skills beyond a basic level. This requires a teacher who can be selfless, knowing, unconventional, and able to dramatically change students for the better, but who can accomplish the change in ways that the students see their own role in the change more than they see the teacher's. Wouldn't this make an excellent definition of the ideal experiential educator? An experiential educator is a leader-facilitator who experientially shares his or her wisdom, knowledge, and vision in selfless, creative, and subtle ways.

## EXPERIENTIAL EDUCATION AND TAO THINKING

The purpose of this book is to investigate what it means to be a Leader Who is Hardly Known. Certainly experiential education and Tao thinking have much in common. An excellent demonstration of that commonality is a passage by Alan Watts in which he compares Taoism and its philosophical complement, Confucianism. I, however, invite the reader to look at the passage twice. In the first reading, read the passage as is it is written. In the second reading, mentally replace Confucianism with "traditional education" and Taoism with "experiential education." I think the substitution will make perfect sense.

> When we turn to ancient Chinese society, we find two "philosophical" traditions playing complementary parts - Confucianism and Taoism. Generally speaking, the former concerns itself with the linguistic, ethical, legal, and ritual conventions which provide society with its system of communication. Confucianism, in other words, preoccupies itself with conventional knowledge, and under its auspices children are brought up so

*their originally wayward and whimsical natures are made to fit the Procrustean bed of the social order.... Taoism, on the other hand,... concerns itself with unconventional knowledge, with the understanding of life directly, instead of in the abstract, linear terms of representational thinking. Confucianism presides, then, over the socially necessary task of forcing the original spontaneity of life into the rigid rules of convention - a task which involves not only conflict and pain, but also the loss of that peculiar naturalness and un-self-consciousness for which little children are so much loved, and which is sometimes regained by saints and sages. The function of Taoism is to undo the inevitable damage of this discipline, and not only to restore but also to develop the original spontaneity, which is termed "tzu-jan" or self-so-ness.*[5]

If the opening reference to "ancient Chinese society" was replaced with the phrase, "the history of educational theory," Watts would have unknowingly written an explanation of traditional vs. experiential education that rivals anything that I have ever read.

*The Leader Who is Hardly Known* is a series of short essays about leadership in experiential education. Somewhat in the style of the ancient Taoist classic, *Chuangtze*, each essay begins with a story about a great teacher (in this instance, a teacher called The Leader Who is Hardly Known). The story is followed by a discussion that uses Tao thought and Tao quotations to shed light on the specific issues brought up by the story.

Each essay stands on its own, and the reader can leaf through the book and pick chapters at random. The book, however, does have an order, as chapters are arranged in four sections. Section One is "A Good Start" and includes five chapters about personality traits that affect leadership. Section Two is "Teaching Tips" and consists of four chapters about common experiential education programming elements. Section Three is "The Role of Nature," which looks at humanity's connection to the natural world. Section Four is the conclusion. The chapters are intentionally short and fairly straightforward, and the reader can determine for him or herself whether the point of the chapter coincides with his or her philosophy of experiential education.

Philosophy, by its very nature, is fairly hazy and theoretical. While I enjoy theory and haziness, and enjoy it more and more with each passing year, I am suspicious of any education book that totally lacks practicality. Therefore, I attempt to infuse some of the nuts and bolts of experiential education into what is largely a theoretical text. Actual situations in the field of experiential education often are used as examples, and at times, specific solutions to very concrete problems are suggested.

The Taoist references in the book are not restricted to the *Tao Te Ching*. Translations of other ancient Taoist writings also are sources of information. They include *Chuangtze, Huainanzi,* and *Hua Hu Ching. Chuangtze* often is viewed as a companion piece to the *Tao Te Ching*. Written by Chuangtze and followers of Chuangtze about two hundred years after the *Tao Te Ching*, its parables and monologues expound on the sometime confusing text of Lao-tzu's original work. *Huainanzi* is a collection of writings by Taoist scholars during the Han Dynasty (around the 2nd Century BC), and the *Hua Hu Ching* is a second, largely unknown work credited to Lao-tzu. In addition to ancient Chinese classics, contemporary interpretations of the Eastern thought also are used, including works by Alan Watts, Lin Yutang, and Krishnamurti.

## THE INTENDED AUDIENCE FOR THE BOOK

*The Leader Who is Hardly Known* is written for the full range of people who consider themselves experiential educators. That includes ropes course facilitators, wilderness trip leaders, interpretative naturalists, camp counselors, recreation professionals, corporate trainers, coaches, service-learning coordinators, therapeutic recreation specialists, as well as classroom teachers who use experiential methods with their students. I, however, put in an additional stipulation that this book is intended for experiential educators who are in it for the long haul. Many of the fields under the experiential education umbrella, especially those that deal with outdoor adventure and environmental education, have staff who work in experiential education for two or three years, then move on to their "real" careers. This book is for the other folks, those experiential educators who either have gray hair or see themselves staying in experiential education until their hair turns gray.

The fact that I do not direct this book to the short-termers is, by no means, a condemnation of them. The young educators who see leading wilderness trips or teaching children about nature as a transition opportunity are the life and spirit and, most importantly, the passion of experiential education. For a few years, these people ignore long hours and lousy pay because free time and money are not their reasons for doing what they do. The experience itself is the motivating force. These short-termers are the true experiential educators in that they see life as a series of learning opportunities. Like the person who enlists in the military or joins Vista or the Peace Corps, the extended stopover is more a valuable adventure than a job. I often have thought that the very best classroom teachers have to be the people who were first camp counselors, interpretative naturalists, or some other kind of experiential educator. With a passion for learning and a healthy understanding of the limitations of the classroom, these teachers have what most non-classroom experiential educators do not have – an extended period of time with their students. These educators have a real shot at making a positive impact on the people they teach.

Yet in spite of my respect for the transient experiential educator, there are three reasons that I write this book for the career experiential educator. First of all, this book is about developing a personal philosophy of experiential education. While some readers may disagree with me, I think that developing a clear professional philosophy becomes a priority only after a person is competent in the technical aspects of a job. It is just too hard for a person to worry about why they are doing something until they know how to do it. As an example, I have a friend who teaches a university course in wilderness travel. The first time he ever offered the course, he spent the first two weeks covering nature writings about the aesthetic and spiritual benefits of wilderness. That approach came to an end, however, when a student came up to him after class and asked, "When are we going to learn how to build a fire?"

The second reason that this book is for long-term experiential educators is that those who have mastered the basics of a profession need something else to study once the initial learning curve has leveled off. Experiential educators have several options after they have a couple of years of learning under their belts. They can quit and do something else (i.e., become short-termers). They can land an experiential education position with decent salary and benefits and let money and security become important motivating factors. Or they can understand at a deeper level the philosophical underpinnings of why they are doing what they are doing. Put another way, they can 1) fine tune their work, 2) understand better the potential and the value of their work, and 3) keep learning so that the learning curve does not flatten out quite so much. May there always be a core of people who stay in experiential education for a long time, and not only are they adequately paid for their talents, but they also find a multitude of ways to keep the job fresh.

The third reason that this book is for the old timers and too-soon-to-be old timers is simply age. This book is written for experiential educators who have a few miles on them. I mentioned earlier that one of the strengths of transient experiential educators is their passion. In some ways, this strength is also a weakness. In particular, passion can lead to excessive enthusiasm for a particular point of view. The prime example is that many young advocates of experiential education see traditional education as the enemy. They oppose anything that hints of lecture, standardized tests, or classroom walls. This book is a meshing of experiential education and Tao thinking. As such, it is a book of moderation and tolerance. Alan Watts repeatedly describes the Tao as water. Nothing is more powerful, yet nothing is more yielding. While water can move the huge rock that lies its path, its preference is to flow around it.[6]

I hope that experiential education sets lofty goals for its leaders. The profession needs a level of quality that cannot be achieved in a short time span. The notion of a Leader Who is Hardly Known could be such a goal. It may be a bit romantic, the stuff of movies like *Dead Poets' Society* and *Mr. Holland's Opus*, but this puts a life-long goal out there to promote ongoing professional growth. No experiential educator will ever fully achieve wisdom, vision, creativity, selflessness, and subtlety - but most would like to be closer to those excellent qualities than they are now.

Twentieth century philosopher Lin Yutang, in his translation and commentary on the *Tao Te Ching*, wrote:

> *The first reaction of anyone scanning the Book of Tao is laughter; the second reaction, laughter at one's own laughter; and the third, a feeling that this sort of teaching is very much needed today.*[7]

I can only suppose that Philosopher Lin must have had friends who were quicker to laugh than I am. For me, the first reaction to the Chinese classic was anything but laughter. It was more like, "I don't get it." That reaction was followed by, "I now get some of it." The third reaction, which is the one I hold today is, "I'll never understand all of it, but what I do get is very much needed in experiential education."

# SECTION ONE
## A Good Start

humility

A big part of Tao leadership is serving as a role model and mentor, and while it is an exaggeration to say that educators have to change their lives in order to teach according to the Tao, personality and personal value systems cannot be separated from leadership or the art of teaching. The first five chapters of this book look at personality traits consistent with Tao thinking. The section is called "A Good Start" because it addresses five traits that a leader should at least think about if he or she is to have a program with Tao-like components. Before significantly changing a program or altering teaching methodologies, those who want to be the Leader Who is Hardly Known must first go about fine-tuning their leadership personality. The five traits are humility, tolerance, wu-wei (non-action), moderation, and steadiness.

tolerance

wu-wei

moderation

steadiness

HUMILITY

# 1

# The Arrogant Monkey

The paddlers beached their canoes and walked fifty yards down-stream to Beaver Rapids. At breakfast earlier that morning, the leaders had forewarned the participants that this stretch of white-water would be the most difficult of the trip and that they would have to scout it out to see whether it was runnable. The group had been paddling for four days, and all the students were now trained both in paddling skills and in reading water. They correctly identified the only possible route through Beaver Rapids. They also, to a person, felt that their skills were not ready for the diffi-cult ferry that would be necessary to position their canoe for the last of three chutes. All of the students decided to portage.

Two of the trip's leaders, however, decided to run the rapids. They asked the Leader Who is Hardly Known and another paddler to go downstream and serve as a rescue boat. They had another stu-dent positioned on shore with a throw rope. Fortunately none of the precautions were necessary, as the leaders paddled to perfec-tion the route the students had laid out. All the students cheered as the skilled team shot the last rapid and blasted through the last standing wave.

Later that evening Kathy, one of the two trip leaders who had run Beaver Rapids, waited for the Leader Who is Hardly Known to walk away from the group at the campfire. She followed him and said, "I have something to ask you. It is about the rapids Dennis and I ran today. I have seen you canoe many times, and I know your ca-noe skills are better than mine. You would have enjoyed running the rapids, yet you chose to portage with the rest of the group. I am sure that you portaged for a reason, and I suspect that you did it because you did not want to stand out from the group. Is this true, and do you think that I was showing off when I decided to run the rapids? That was not my intent, but it has been bothering me all day."

The Leader Who is Hardly Known smiled at the leader. "Chuangtze tells a great story about showing off.[1] The story begins with the ancient King of Wu boating on the Yangtze River. The river flows past a place called Monkey Mountain. The king and his entourage leave the river and hike up the mountain. They soon see the monkeys for which the mountain is named, and when the monkeys see the king, they drop what they are doing and run off to hide in the deep brush. But one monkey stays. It jumps around and grabs at things to show the king its dexterity. When the king shoots at this monkey, the monkey snatches the arrow out of the air and shakes it at the king. The king then orders his attendants to shoot at the monkey. They bombard the monkey with arrows, and, of course, it is quickly killed.

"The king picks up the dead monkey and hands it to his friend, Yen Pu-i, and says, 'This monkey flaunted its skills and relied on its tricks – and it met with misfortune. Take this as a lesson! Do not exhibit your pride in front of others.'

"Yen Pu-i returns home and goes into training. He rids himself of pride, he learns to wipe any hint of superiority from his face, he always excuses himself from actions that would lead to fame – and at the end of three years he was known throughout his homeland for humility.

"Now you ask me if running the rapids was showing off. That is for you to decide. You are not an arrogant monkey, but neither are you a model of humility. Even if you ran the rapids strictly for fun, you stood out from your students. From what I could tell, the students admired you for it and did not resent your skills. So the question is, does being admired contribute to effective leadership?"

# HUMILITY IN A LEADER

*A phoenix appears but rarely, so it is considered an auspicious omen. Peacocks are always showing off their feathers, so they are taken captive.*[2]

Liu I-ming

If there is a best first step toward being a Leader Who is Hardly Known, it is to become genuinely humble. Humility may be the most prevalent theme in classic Taoist literature. In the *Tao Te Ching* alone, easily a fifth of the chapters remind the reader that humility and modesty are basic to a person who is one with the Tao. For example:

> *As (the wise man) succeeds, he takes no credit;*
> *And just because he does not take it, credit never leaves him.*[3]
>
> *Wealth, status, pride are their own ruin.*
> *To do good, work well, and lie low is the way of the blessing.*[4]
>
> *The Sage does not make a show of himself, hence he shines;*
> *Does not justify himself, hence he becomes known;*
> *Does not boast of his ability, hence he gets his credit;*
> *Does not brandish his success, hence he endures;*
> *Does not compete with anyone, hence no one can compete with him.*[5]

There are another dozen passages in the *Tao Te Ching* that just as explicitly express the same sentiment. Two especially colorful ones are "Humility is the root from which greatness springs,"[6] and "If I can be the world's most humble man, then I can be its highest instrument."[7]

That humility is a component of the Tao cannot be doubted. It is one of the cornerstones of the philosophy. The real question for experiential educators is, "What does that have to do with us?"

## HUMILITY AND EXPERIENTIAL EDUCATION

Taoist thinking, not unlike Greek philosophy, recognizes two significant obstacles to personal contentment and a just society. Those obstacles are the dream of fame and the desire for fortune. Of the two, it is the dream of fame that more often blocks the path for experiential educators.[8]

For those in education, fortune (i.e., money) seldom has been a significant motivating factor. Many, if not most experiential educators, have willingly accepted low salaries to facilitate ropes courses or coordinate service learning or serve as therapeutic recreation specialists. Although experiential educators sometimes complain about their pay, I think that many take some private pride in not letting money entice them to less idealistic work. The fact is that this pride may be somewhat misplaced. It is wonderful that many experiential educators forsake good paying jobs for honorable work, but how great is the sacrifice if a person does not value money that much in the first place? It is a little like a non-smoker giving up cigarettes for Lent. If money is not important, why feel superior for giving it up?

Recently there have been efforts to woo corporate and other wealthy clients to ropes courses, wilderness adventures, and ecotourism excursions, but even these attempts rarely are motivated by greed. People have the right to earn a decent wage for good work, and attempts to tap into corporate money often are an effort to keep an experiential education program afloat. While I personally am disappointed that corporate clients have become a high priority among some experiential education programs, it is laughable to think of someone going into the profession for the money.

The dream of fame, however, is a different matter. Fame, in this instance, is not movie star/professional athlete-type notoriety. It is wanting to be admired, it is encouraging devotion from others, it is behaving in certain ways because it impresses other people. It is not so blatant as showing off, but it is doing something in the hope of being recognized. As I sit here and write this chapter, I wonder how much of my effort is motivated by the joy of writing and the need to understand the Tao, and how much is a hope that, by writing a book, I will receive a bit of recognition from my colleagues.

Lin Yutang points out that many people who have been able to escape the lure of wealth still want fame. He cites a monk who tells his student, "It is easier to get rid of the desire for money than to get rid of the desire for fame. Even retired scholars and monks still want to be distinguished and well-known among their company. They want to give public discourses to a large audience, and not retire to a small monastery talking to one pupil." [9]

## Being Hardly Known

In experiential education, I do not know of anyone who does not enjoy being liked and admired by the students he or she serves. Because experiential educators work closely with their students to nurture trust and mutual respect, it is fairly easy to develop a following. It also is easy to bathe in the light of the admiration that that following gives off. Chapter 17 of the *Tao Te Ching*, however, states that the leader who is loved and admired is only the second best kind of leader. The very best leader is the one who is hardly known:

> *The highest type of ruler is one whose existence the people are*
> *barely aware.*
> *Next comes one whom they love and praise.*
> *Next comes one whom they fear.*
> *Next comes one whom they despise and defy.* [10]

If anyone familiar with experiential education was asked whether most experiential educators were praised, feared, despised, or barely known by their students, praised would be the obvious response. Wilderness leaders, interpretative naturalists, recreation program leaders often are praised as great people with great enthusiasm running great programs.

Most experiential educators who are loved and praised are doing a very good job. They serve as leaders, as mentors, and as role models. Still these loved and praised leaders have a responsibility to gradually take their leadership to the next level and to become leaders who are hardly known. This effort, however, is gradual and progressive. In part, the progression is on the part of the students being served. Some groups may initially need leaders to offer concrete guidance, and such overt leadership leads to admiration. Only with clear direction in the early stages of a program can individuals within a group learn to lead themselves. As participants gradually assume leadership responsibility, designated leaders fade into the background.

More significantly, however, the progression away from admiration takes place in the frame of mind and the actions of the educators themselves. New leaders, inexperienced leaders, may need some re-affirmation from a group that they are doing a good job. They need a sense that they are in charge and are doing something to mold the education of the people they serve. Just as the students need to develop a sense of self-esteem, so too do the leaders. It is normal to want confirmation from others that a good job is being done.

With maturity, however, external recognition of good work becomes less important. Affirmation becomes internalized. Intelligent leaders who continue to improve themselves know they do good work without surrounding themselves with an admiration society. Genuine humility is not a person thinking he or she is less than anyone else. It is going through life without having to have his or her good work publicly acknowledged by others.

Contemporary writers Chungliang Al Huang and Jerry Lynch describe a series of attributes associated with Tao teaching. They put humility alongside of self-acceptance and observe that humility comes only with self-acceptance. In their book, *Mentoring*, they write, "Taoist thought encourages us to be all that we have been given, yet act as if we have received nothing. In this way, no one will be aware of us yet we will bring happiness to all."[11]

In the introduction to this book, I wrote that this book was intended for leaders and facilitators who plan on making experiential education their career. One reason for this is the time and profes-

sional maturity it takes to reach genuine humility. It takes practice, conscious effort, and years in the field for a competent leader
to wean himself or herself of the praise of others. Praise and admiration are enticing, especially so because a leader can be very,
very good without having to give it up. It may seem like an unnecessary sacrifice to give up the praise if the improvement in leadership is only incremental. There might be a handful of innately
humble people who are so at peace with themselves that they
never need external confirmation of their worth, but most of us
have to pass through a period of "positive strokes" before we have
the self-esteem to go it on our own. Like so much else, this requires maturation. Once comfortable with ourselves, we can consciously take steps to make sure that recognition falls not on us,
but on other staff and on the participants.

Tao thinking sometimes describes this maturation toward humility
not as gaining humility, but of getting rid of pride and arrogance.
As Lui I-ming described it, "In the case of developed people, the
loftier their path becomes the more humble their hearts are. Their
virtue grows day by day, yet they become more circumspect, until
all pride is gone and all agitation is dissolved."[12]

Hua-Ching Ni goes so far as to describe the achievement of humility as getting rid of a sickness. Ni lists a range of illnesses that affect humanity, many of them involving excessive pride. His list
includes:

- To brag about your own achievements is sick.
- To bend your own virtuous principles for popular
  interests is sick.
- To allure and entice the naive is sick.
- To take pride in your honor and glory is sick.
- To please with, or be pleased by, flattery is sick.
- To take pride in your own high virtue is sick.
- To think that you are superior to all others is sick.
- To be self-righteous is sick.[13]

## A Concrete Step

An interesting question on the topic of humility is whether an experiential educator needs to be truly humble or can simply behave humbly when leading a group. Most experiential educators already have a persona. They turn on the charm when leading groups, and usually that charm is convincing. Their enthusiasm kicks into a higher gear, and personal problems get put aside as much as possible. In my own leadership, I have been told by co-facilitators that I change my tone of voice when in front of groups, but this is something that I am not even conscious of. So can an experiential educator "get humble" when humility is called for?

I think that the answer to that question is probably "no." Most people are not good enough actors to feign humility. Still "acting" humble may not be a bad first step. Even if orchestrated, humble behavior may lead to genuine humility. By this I mean that conscious acts of humility will help a person become humble in the same way that orchestrated enthusiasm in front of groups makes educators less self-conscious and more extroverted in everyday life. Acting humble may be analogous to sitting alone in a quiet room. Sitting quietly is not necessarily meditation, but it is closer to meditation than most people get, and it is a good first step toward meditating.

If humility does not come naturally, it makes sense to do things that make the leadership of a program more humble. The following are a couple of suggestions:

Lesson 1: Take conscious steps to divert credit to others. In assertiveness training, people learn to accept compliments without minimizing them. For a person with assertiveness training, the proper response to a compliment about good work is "Thank you," not "Oh, it was nothing." From a perspective of a leader who is hardly known, however, the proper response to a compliment is not to graciously accept the kind words, but to divert the credit to another deserving person. When, for example, a group thanks the leader for a particularly good activity, the leader turns the compliment back on the group. When a journalist wants a photograph or quote for a feature article that will appear in a local newspaper, the leader passes that privilege on to someone else who will benefit from the recognition. Even when a leader is uniquely qualified to lead a program or present at a conference, he or she conducts that program or presentation in such a way that others will share the credit for a job well done.

I once wrote an article with a good friend of mine. While my friend did over half of the work on the initial manuscript, I made all of the revisions and had all of the correspondence with the editor of the journal where the article was to appear. When the article was published, the editorial staff of the journal forgot to include my friend as co-author. When I sheepishly called my friend on the telephone to explain that his name did not appear on the article, his immediate and genuine response was, "It doesn't matter. The important thing was to get our thoughts out there." My friend teaches at a university, an institution where prestige on campus extensively depends on the number of publications that can be racked up. Still he was not concerned that his name was not associated with the article. How many of us are so altruistic that we are willing to do good things without caring about getting the credit?

LESSON 2: LEARN TO SAY "I DON'T KNOW."
This is a small thing, but experiential educators too seldom say, "I don't know." For some, it is not wanting to appear ignorant. For others, it is not wanting to leave a student's question unresolved. When it is not realistic to search out the answer from a library or from a person who might know the answer, there is a temptation to provide an off-the-cuff answer. Unfortunately giving a "best shot" answer can become the knee-jerk response. The preface to the answer is "I am not sure, but if I had to guess, I would say...." And out comes an answer, even if a half hour later, the gut feeling of the leader is that he or she really winged it on that one. Being comfortable with not knowing is an acquired skill, a blend of humility and self-esteem.

Being comfortable with not knowing also is a sign of a great teacher. For example, Confucius was once asked by a couple of boys whether the sun was closer to the earth when it was just rising or when it was directly overhead at noon. One of the boys argued that because the sun was bigger at dawn, it must be nearer at dawn. The other boy said that because the sun is warmer at noon, it must be nearer at noon. Confucius told the boys that he did not know which argument was correct. The boys laughed at Confucius, saying, "Who said you were so smart?"[14]

包容

TOLERANCE

# 2

# The Obsessed Rock Climber

The Leader Who is Hardly Known was making a presentation at an experiential education conference. He began by saying, "I would like to begin this workshop with a short lecture on processing techniques. I do so, because...."

Immediately a young woman in the audience threw up her hand and began to speak without waiting to be acknowledged. "Excuse me," she said, "but is this going to be a lecture? I do not mean to be rude, but if this is going to be a lecture, I would like to leave now so that I can attend a different session. Experiential education should be done, not listened to."

The Leader Who is Hardly Known responded to the woman. "If this workshop does not meet your needs, I hope that you leave the session and attend another. Experiential education works only when students take some of the responsibility for their learning. Before you leave, however, please listen to a story. The story is short and will take only a couple of minutes. [*]

> "There once was an experiential educator who delighted in rock climbing. He surrounded himself with talented climbers, and he worked hard to improve his climbing skills. He became so engrossed in rock climbing that he let it affect his teaching. Unless his programs involved climbing, he merely went through the motions. Even when the programs included climbing, he had little patience for students who were not as excited about the sport as he was. The experi-

---

[*] Some experiential educators dislike lectures, but enjoy stories. That is an interesting distinction. Either lecturers should become better storytellers or listeners should become better at seeing the stories in a lecture.

ential educator's assistant became so worried about her mentor that she offered a reward to anyone who could convince the experiential educator to curb his obsession.

"The assistant's best friend said that if anyone could influence a teacher, it would be another teacher. The friend suggested Chuangtze, and the assistant immediately asked her friend to go to Chuangtze with a plea for help and the offer of a reward – and although the sage scoffed at the reward, he did agree to talk to the assistant about the problem.

"When the assistant had one look at Chuangtze, however, she knew that the plan would not work. She apologized to Chuangtze for wasting his time, but explained to him that the experiential educator only took time to talk to rock climbers.

"'This is not a problem,' said Chuangtze, 'for I am an excellent climber.'

"'Even so,' responded the assistant, 'my mentor only sees rock climbers who look like rock climbers. They are scruffy, they wear helmets, and their t-shirts have the sleeves ripped off. They have a rock jock look in their eyes. You have the words and the wardrobe of a scholar, and that won't get you to my supervisor's campfire.'

"'Then get me the clothes of a climber,' said Chuangtze. 'Get me spandex, get me Goretex, get me a helmet and a harness. I can dress to climb.' Then Chuangtze went three days without shaving. He worked on a tan. He scraped up his knuckles and put on climbing shoes. Finally he donned climbing gear and had the assistant introduce him to the experiential educator.

"'Who are you,' said the experiential educator, 'that you would have my assistant introduce you to me?'

"'I am a climber,' said Chuangtze, 'and I think that I have something to teach you. I am sure that I know of some mountain ascents that will challenge you as no others.'

"'Really? I am always looking for mountains that will test and hone my climbing skills. Tell me about them.'

"'There are three. One of them is the Mountain of the Son of Heaven. Another is the Mountain of the Great Teacher. The third is the Mountain of the Ordinary Person.'

"'What is the Mountain of the Son of Heaven like?' asked the experiential educator.

"'Its route is the most difficult of all. The Mountain of the Son of Heaven has the four seasons as its base. It has the enduring heart as its rock face and Yin and Yang as its handholds and footholds. Its peak is virtue and sound judgment. Reach its first ledge and nothing stands before you. Reach its summit and none will rise above you. Climb this mountain once and enlightenment is yours.'

"The experiential educator was confused, thought perhaps he was speaking to a fool, but he asked, 'The Mountain of the Great Teacher, what about it?'

"'The Mountain of the Great Teacher,' said Chuangtze, 'has knowledge and patience as its base, honesty and integrity as its rock face, loyalty and compassion as its footholds and handholds, wisdom at its peak. Reach its first ledge and you harmonize with the song in the hearts of students, bringing guidance to their confused path. Reach its summit, you are light like the sun, moon, and stars. Climb it once and all the world will learn from your example.'

"'And what of the Mountain of the Ordinary Person?' asked the experiential educator.

"'The Mountain of the Ordinary Person is quite ordinary. It has compacted soil at its base, climber's chalk at each of its handholds, and countless climbers scurrying across its rock face. Reach its first ledge and you stand where a previous climber has peed. Reach its summit, and there is a momentary sense of pride and accomplishment. Climb this mountain once, and you have something to talk about over beers.

"'The Mountain of the Ordinary Person is a mountain, and all mountains possess great beauty. But a great teacher has the chance to be a Son of Heaven, yet you are addicted to the mountains of ordinary people. I dare to suggest that you have greater mountains to climb.'"[1]

The Leader Who is Hardly Known finished the story, then turned to the woman who wanted to leave. "There are several good points to this story," he said. "One is about obsession. Another is about finding the Way. A third is even about assessing people by their dress and appearance. You, however, introduced me to another lesson in the story – one I had not considered before. An experiential educator can be surrounded by activity and by people doing things, but he still needs to be open to all avenues of learning, even lecture.

"I apologize for putting you on the spot in front of other people, but by the way that you were able to voice your opinion about experiential education, I sense you are mature enough to not take my comments personally. I am reminding myself and talking to everyone in this room when I say that a good education is one that comes in many forms."

 TOLERANCE

*The wise leave the road and find the Way; fools cling to the Way and lose the road.*[2]

Huainanzi

One of the most frequently quoted truisms of experiential education is "Tell me, I will forget; show me, I will remember; let me do it, and

I will understand." I, like most experiential educators, had encountered the quote many times, both in print and in oral presentations, but I never knew where it came from. Once or twice I'd seen it identified as an "ancient Chinese proverb," but that did little to help narrow the source. Therefore when I read a similar quote in a collection of ancient Taoist writings called the *Huainanzi*, I wondered whether I had stumbled across the quote's origins. The *Huainanzi* passage, however, did not carry the exact same meaning as its more famous counterpart, for it read:

> To recite the books of ancient kings is not as good as hearing
> their words.
> Hearing their words is not as good as attaining that whereby
> those words were spoken.
> To attain whereby those words were spoken is something that
> words cannot say.
> Therefore, "a way that can be spoken is not the eternal Way."[3]

This quote does not roll off the tongue quite as easily as "Tell me, I will forget...," but I actually like it better. Instead of saying that a certain style of teaching does not work very well, it is gentler and more accurate in simply observing that teaching methods have limits. It says that learning from the written and spoken word can set a student in the right direction, but it cannot lead to deep and full understanding. Only personal and direct experience can do that.

What an intelligent and reasonable way to state a basic premise of experiential education! Lectures, texts, and other forms of traditional education may establish groundwork for direct experience, but until experiential learning occurs, there will not be understanding at the level that exists in those who do the lecturing and the writing. Once lectures and books have primed the pump, it becomes the role of experiential educators to facilitate the students' initial efforts into experiential learning. Such a collaborative relationship between traditional and experiential education is more inclusive, more tolerant, and more progressive than an approach that pits one methodology against another.

## Intolerance Toward Traditional Education

The overall purpose of this chapter is to discuss tolerance in experiential education. This, of course, is a broad issue and encompasses a range of topics. I, however, would like to begin with only one of those topics–tolerance in the relationship between traditional and experiential education. Experiential educators, as a whole, have a tolerant nature, but sometimes have a blind spot when it comes to traditional education. Some experiential educators who are not themselves classroom teachers criticize traditional education. At best, these detractors perceive traditional education as ineffective. At worst, they see it as part of an institutional system that saps spontaneity out of students and makes them compliant citizens in an established power structure. Even when traditional school systems do something out of the ordinary, such as establishing a charter school, a school-to-work program, or a Montessori kindergarten in a public school, there is a sense of "yeah, but that's experiential education." And when experiential education in the schools becomes the norm (e.g., climbing walls in the gymnasium), there is a mild acknowledgement that traditional education is finally catching on.

Some of this aversion to traditional education may be the direct expression of people who were dissatisfied with their own formal education, but I think that the issue runs deeper than that. It may, in fact, be an inherent weakness in experiential education itself. I say this, not because experiential educators overall are not open-minded, but because a couple of the strengths of the experiential education profession are also attributes that can lead to selective intolerance. A prime example is experiential education's relative youthfulness. Not only is the profession itself still maturing, but the members of the profession tend to be young. For the most part, this is a good thing. In many ways, experiential education is still grappling with its exact niche in society, and as a result, the profession is alive and ever-changing. And because its membership has a large core of people who are young in age, there is an energy and enthusiasm to complement the vibrancy of the profession. Youth, however, may lack the perspective that comes with experience. I write this book as a forty-eight year old man who would not mind reliving some of his younger years, but simultaneously I appreciate that one of the lessons that comes with a half century of living is a slowness to judge others. Youth's strength is its passion, but this passion sometimes makes it hard to walk in another person's shoes.

A second strength of experiential education that can lead to intolerance is its fringe position when compared to traditional education. Traditional education is the mainstream institution, experiential education the outsider. This fringe position is the home of innovation, but it also can be a place of self-righteousness. Being on the outside looking in, it is easy to see the flaws of the mainstream and feel superior. The fringe also can be a place so distant from the norm that communication is limited to other people also on the fringe. This leads to self-pollination, where an ideology seems right merely because the small group who adheres to the ideology speaks only to each other.

One entity that is *not* the source of intolerance toward traditional education is experiential education philosophy and theory. John Dewey and Kurt Hahn, unlike some contemporary experiential educators, had at least one foot in traditional education. Dewey, in particular, saw experiential education and the traditional classroom as two parts of one system and actually criticized wholesale rejection of traditional education by those who espoused the values of direct experience:

> It is not too much to say that an educational philosophy which professes to be based on the idea of freedom may be as dogmatic as ever was the traditional education which it reacted against.... We may reject knowledge of the past as the end of education and thereby only emphasize its importance as a means. When we do that we have a problem that is new in the story of education: How shall the young become acquainted with the past in such a way that the acquaintance is a potent agent in appreciation of the living present?[4]

There has been intelligent rhetoric suggesting that attempts to integrate experiential education into traditional schools is not a constructive use of time.[5] The argument is that the inertia and

bureaucracy of traditional education, combined with the significant differences in the two philosophies, doom such efforts to
only marginal success. Proponents of this point of view suggest
that experiential education should concentrate on separate, but
complementary, endeavors providing educational opportunities
outside of the classroom and outside of normal school hours.

This perspective makes sense, at least for a segment of the experiential education profession, only so long as the complementary
aspect is recognized. Non-classroom experiential education cannot replace traditional classroom education, nor should it even try.
In Taoist terms, experiential and traditional education, when each
is done well, serve two different educational needs and make for a
well-rounded education. To even think of experiential education
and traditional education as somehow in competition with each
other is to fail to recognize that students benefit from both.


## CONSCIOUS TOLERANCE

In the ideal, tolerance is not so much a conscious goal of welcoming diversity as it is an almost effortless result of humility and self-
acceptance. When a person has nothing to prove to anyone else,
an opposing perspective is not a threat. In fact, from a Taoist perspective, if not for a we vs. them mentality, there would be no need
to guard against intolerance at all. When a person is truly humble,
the thought of condemning another person's actions or ideas is
not the natural way of reacting. In the *Hua Hu Ching*, a relatively
unknown Taoist work credited to Lao-tzu, the master explains to
his student that tolerance, while important, is only an issue for
those who have yet to find the Way:

> ...tolerance is a necessary virtue in everyone's daily life, but for
> a universal integral being there is nothing that needs to be tol-
> erated or labeled as tolerance. Tolerance exists only in the
> relative sphere. Why is this? If someone does something un-
> pleasant to us, we need to gather our strength to bear it; it is
> a difficult and disagreeable situation. However, if you have
> risen above the relative concepts of the mind, there is no self

*and others, no longevity or brevity, no life or death in your
mind, so there is no hatred or resentment. What, then, is the
necessity for tolerance?* [6]

The point to be made here is not that experiential education should
stop being passionate and innovative. I am not even sure to what
extent experiential education should shift its position from the
fringe of the education spectrum. These attributes are some of experiential education's greatest strengths. The *Chuangtze* even includes passion, innovation, and an outsider's perspective as key
characteristics of those "who wish to bring peace to the world, who
teach and instruct, who pursue learning at home and abroad." De-
spite this, the *Chuangtze* goes on to warn that these exact same attributes can just as easily lead to arrogance, resentful slandering of
others, and a pride in being different without considering whether
the difference is an improvement.[7]

If experiential education, as a profession, has the potential for intolerance, individual experiential educators must make a conscious
and continuous effort to counter that tendency. This applies to attitudes toward traditional education and, perhaps even more so, to a
broader range of social issues. Many experiential educators are
supporters of various social causes (e.g., cultural diversity, environmental preservation, women's rights, gay rights, and the rights of
people with disabilities) which, if taken to an extreme, can lead to an
intolerance of people who do not feel the same. This lends itself to
a position of "I'll be tolerant, so long as you agree with me."

An excellent model of tolerance is the story that Dan Garvey told
in his 1997 Kurt Hahn Address.[8] In the speech, Dan told the story
of walking along the edge of a natural area with a friend of his.
They hear the pounding of drums and move toward the sound. In
a small clearing, they discover a red-haired, blue-eyed man in an
Indian headdress leading a small group through a Native American ceremony. The two men watch for a few minutes, then quietly
walk away. Dan's friend is McClellan Hall, a Cherokee Indian, director of the Indian Youth Leadership Project, and a man who has
written about why it is not appropriate for Anglos to conduct Native rituals. Quite naturally, Dan asks Mac why he did not say

something to the group – the ceremony must have been distasteful to Mac's values. Mac's response was that speaking up would have served no useful purpose, but would have in some way diminished the leader's integrity.

Perhaps for McClellan Hall, such tolerance comes naturally. Part of his personality may be to not let ideology justify harming or embarrassing other people. Others of us may not be so fortunate. With the equivalence of road rage, our first instinct sometimes is to counter an injustice with retribution – and if the perpetrator of the injustice is embarrassed, so much the better.

Conscious and continuous tolerance, however, need not be a demanding task. It is little more than thinking before acting and acknowledging that there is more than one way to think, more than one way to do something. Just as experiential education in its perfect form is accepting and nurturing of diversity in people, conscious and continuous tolerance asks us to be open to the many different ways of doing things. The *Huainanzi* is explicit about this topic:

> It is necessary to win people's hearts. To be able to win
> people's hearts, it is necessary to have self-mastery. To be ca-
> pable of self-mastery, it is necessary to be flexible.... Sages use
> culture to communicate with society and use reality to do
> what is appropriate. They are not bound to one track; they do
> not stagnate or neglect to adapt. This is why their failures are
> few and their successes are many, why their directives are car-
> ried out and no one can deny them.[9]

Tolerance does not mean letting every injustice slide, nor being wimpy, too scared or too apathetic to stand up for what is right. Conversely, it also does not mean becoming frazzled every time something bothersome occurs, and seldom does it mean protesting in a knee-jerk fashion. Krishnamurti suggests that there are two kinds of protest. One is mere reaction to something disliked; the usual result is a rejection of the established orthodoxy by becoming a disciple of a new orthodoxy. In this case, one narrow thought pattern replaces another. The other kind of protest is consistent with tolerance, and that Krishnamurti calls "intelligent revolt." This response is not simply rejection based upon a distaste for something, but a clear understanding of what is tasteful or important in each individual situation as it arises. In Krishnamurti's own words:

> ... there is an intelligent revolt which is not a reaction, and which comes with self-knowledge through the awareness of one's own thought and feeling. It is only when we face experience as it comes and do not avoid disturbance that we keep intelligence highly awakened; and intelligence highly awakened is intuition, which is the only true guide in life. [10]

## CONCLUDING STORY

In the early 1980s I directed a residential outdoor education center in the redwoods south of San Francisco. Fifth and sixth-graders came to the center for a week to study natural history and environmental awareness. One of my responsibilities was to conduct evaluation sessions with the classroom teachers on the last day of their schools' visit. One of the teachers' most common complaints was the frequent physical contact that the naturalist staff had with one another. If two staff members were standing next to each other, odds were that they would have an arm around each other. Often they were in an arm-and-arm chain of three or four people.

In my two years at the center, the staff never dealt with the complaint. To my recollection, we never even seriously considered why the teachers were bothered by the physical contact. Our reaction was that these teachers had serious hang-ups about physical closeness, and that it was the teachers' problem, not ours. We felt that the teachers came from the unfriendly atmosphere of traditional schools and were jealous that we worked in a place where people liked and trusted each other.

Viewing the situation in the context of tolerance, I now see that the staff of the outdoor education center was wrong. When with students, we preached "emotional safety." Students were told that nature camp was an environment where people could freely express their feelings and opinions, knowing that they would be listened to in a non-judgmental way. Likewise, with the teachers, we set up an evaluative process, but in retrospect, it was a bit of a sham. At least on the issue of physical contact between staff, we barely listened to the teachers and, behind their backs, were judgmental.

If the teachers misinterpreted our actions, then so too might have the students. At the very least, we were creating an unnecessary barrier between us and the teachers, and these teachers were the people who were going to carry the environmental messages of the nature center back to the classroom. How far would that message carry if the teachers thought that the messengers were oddballs who constantly hugged trees and each other? We as a staff would have been more effective *as educators* had we considered the teachers' position and eased up on the physical contact. More importantly, we would have been better people had we been more tolerant of their feelings.

WU-WEI

# 3

# The Foxes of Isle Royale

The Leader Who is Hardly Known took a group of five students backpacking on Lake Superior's Isle Royale. Halfway through the trip, the excursion was going well, with one of the highlights being exceptional wildlife watching. In four days, the group already had good looks at moose, beaver, Canada jays, broad-winged hawks, ospreys, and loons. They hadn't seen any wolves, but there had been tracks around their tents when they woke up on the third morning.

On the fourth day, the group hiked over the granite spine of the island and made camp at McCargoe Cove. Being early September, the summer crowds were gone, and the Leader Who is Hardly Known was pleased to find that they had the backcountry campground to themselves. At dusk, a pair of red foxes scampered into camp. Unafraid, they came right up to the group and started begging for food like a couple of lap dogs.

The students had been trained in minimum impact and knew better than to feed the wildlife. They were, however, overcome by the cuteness and the persistence of the foxes. "Can we feed them?" they asked.

The Leader Who is Hardly Known looked at the foxes and said, "You know my feelings about feeding wildlife, and you know the rules of the park. I think that you also know that I will not feed them. In fact, I am tempted to chase them away with pebbles, except that I do not have the heart. Still I leave the decision up to you. Other backpackers have made beggars of these two, and realistically I don't think your actions will change their habits one way or the other. Act according to your own conscience."

The Leader Who is Hardly Known then dawdled a minute or two, left the campsite, and wandered down toward the water. Although he walked nearly a hundred yards, the evening was still and voices carried to the rock where he sat. Someone must have tossed some food for the foxes, because he heard clearly, "Hey butthead, knock it off!"

Then another voice responded, "He said I could do what I wanted. If I want to feed them, I can feed them."

"Don't be dense," said the first voice. "It's a test. He wants to see if we'll do what he wants us to. So knock it off. Somebody finally doesn't treat you like a dweeb, and you still want to piss him off."

"It's just a piece of peanut butter bread."

"Well, just don't do it."

The next morning, just as the group broke camp and stepped back onto the trail, Sammy, one of the students on the trip, came up to the Leader Who is Hardly Known, "I suppose you know we gave the foxes some bread last night. Are you disappointed?"

"No, I was serious when I said that the decision was yours. I'm a teacher and rarely a cop. Last night was a lesson. Did you learn anything?"

"No, I don't think I learned anything," said Sammy. "It's more like I got a feeling that we screwed up a little bit. You told us about the rule of not feeding animals, and we went and did it anyway."

"It falls on you to decide whether you failed last night, just as it falls on me to decide whether I should have even given you the chance to feed the foxes when I knew it could be bad for them. But that's the beauty of time spent in nature. She is always giving us..."

The Leader Who is Hardly Known stopped speaking in mid-sentence, for just then he saw a fox coming around a bend in the trail and heading straight for them. The fox carried a dead rabbit in its mouth. It trotted to within ten feet of the Leader Who is Hardly

Known, came to a momentary stop, then turned right and disappeared through a break in the thimbleberries.

The student laughed. "That fox has more guts than me! It just told you to stick it."

The Leader Who is Hardly Known nodded. "Ordinarily I would say that you are wrong, that this fine hunter is beyond caring about what I think, and we just happened to be in the way. Still the lesson that just came to me is so perfect that it cannot be coincidence. Had I been more open, I would have learned it last night, but this fellow had to come by and give it to me again."

"You just learned something from that fox?" asked Sammy.

"Yes, I did. And I'll tell you what I learned, but first tell me if you learned anything."

"I learned," said Sammy, "that foxes that hunt are even cooler than foxes that beg."

"That is what I learned, too," said the Leader Who is Hardly Known. "Do you think that it says anything to you personally?"

"Yeah, it says that I won't feed foxes any more. And I'll stop not because you told me to, but because I want foxes to be more like that one."

"That, in itself, is a good lesson," said the Leader Who is Hardly Known, "but that's not what I meant to ask. Do you think that the way that this fox lives tells you anything about the way you ought to live?"

Sammy took a moment to think about the question. "Ah, not really. I guess it says that it is better for me to be a hunter than a beggar, but I'm not a hunter or a beggar."

"Well done. That is a good interpretation. Let me tell you my interpretation, because I think we're thinking the same thing. Do you remember last night how tempting it was to feed the foxes?"

"Well, yeah! We did it even though we knew you'd get mad."

"Right," said the Leader Who is Hardly Known. "For me, that is how tempting it is to teach in a way that makes students like and admire me. If I help them a lot, they think I am good. Other teachers think I am good. Even I think that I'm good. If I am not careful though, it makes students dependent."

"You mean like little beggars," said the student.

"Willing to take the easy way out," replied the Leader Who is Hardly Known. "But I wouldn't blame the students any more than I blamed the foxes last night. My job is to figure out how to do as little as possible, but still have students learn. I have to help when you really need help, to not help when you don't. I find that line very hard to hold, and because I like being needed, I sometimes do too much."

"So you think that we like you too much? How weird, we finally get a teacher we respect, and you tell me it's wrong."

"No, it's not wrong. I just need one of you to shake a dead rabbit in my face every once in awhile."

"Don't worry," said Sammy. "Before the end of the trip, I'll do my best to tell you that you're no help at all."

"And if you don't need my help," said the Leader Who is Hardly Known, "I will thank you for it."

 WU-WEI

*Wu Wei is the Watercourse Way, as one acts from the heart and follows nature's flow, just as when leaves fall, they follow the wind, land in water, and go with the flow.*[1]

Chungliang Al Huang and Jerry Lynch

Loren Eisely once wrote "If there is magic on this planet, it is contained in water."[2] I don't think that there is a Tao equivalent to Eiseley's quote, but if there was, it might read, "If there is Tao on this planet, it is in the watercourse."[3] In Taoist writings, the flow of water repeatedly is used as a metaphor for the Tao. In the *Tao Te Ching*, for example, the watercourse way symbolizes both the humility and the power of the Tao. The Tao is the Way of nature, very powerful, yet always seeking the path of least resistance. Because it seeks the path of least resistance, nothing can overcome it. It supports all life, yet constantly seeks to lower itself below all other things. Nature is one with the Tao, and nowhere is it more apparent than in water.[4]

Humans, unfortunately, do not move with the Tao as effortlessly as water. People tend to resist when pushed and continually strive to elevate their position. This, of course, does not mean that humans cannot be as the watercourse, moving with a natural flow in both their lives and their leadership. It just means that it does not come naturally, so humans must consciously act in a manner consistent with the watercourse way. The Chinese have a word for this, and it is called "wu-wei."

Wu-wei, while not as familiar a concept to Westerners as either "Tao" or "yin and yang," is key to Tao thinking. According to Alan Watts, it is "after the Tao (itself), the second important principle of Taoism."[5] Often wu-wei is translated into English as "non-action," but this is more a literal translation than a useful working definition. "Wei" means to do or to act out, and "wu" means no or not, so "wu-wei" does translate as non-action or no action. Yet wu-wei does not mean doing nothing. Doing nothing connotes laziness, apathy, and a failure to complete a task, and wu-wei does not mean any of these things. Wu-wei is accomplishing the task with as little effort as possible, because if done correctly, little effort is all that is required. It is the difference between confronting a charging attacker by tackling him head on or taking advantage of the attacker's momentum in a judo move. Wu-wei is not "not doing." Rather it is "not forcing."[6] Blackney describes it as the human action that complements the Tao of nature. Whereas the Tao is the path or the way of nature, wu-wei is the human stillness that allows the Tao to act through a person without hindrance.[7]

## THE WU-WEI LEADER

An experiential educator reading this description might say that experiential education is consistent with wu-wei. Experiential educators want to "not act" when the group they are serving can accomplish a task on their own. Competent teachers want to set their students on a path consistent with the Way, then step back as the experience does the teaching and opens the door to new experiences. Still the match is not exact. The following is a more detailed look at wu-wei. It will address three aspects of the philosophy of non-action and discuss whether they are a part of experiential education as well. The three aspects are 1) not wanting to be needed, 2) living and leading by non-contrivance, and 3) maturing toward wu-wei.

### WU-WEI MEANS NOT WANTING TO BE NEEDED.
The ultimate goal of facilitated experiential education is to have the educator become unnecessary. As students move through an experience, the instructor mentors them so they can encounter future experiences on their own. The educator may remain in the minds of students as a role model or as a person who is available in a crisis, but the ideal end result, in both experiential and traditional education, is for students to mature to a point where facing new situations is done as self-sufficient individuals. In a perfect world, educators work themselves out of a job.

On this matter, the Tao is consistent with experiential education. It is, in fact, the heart of the leader-who-is-hardly-known concept.[8] According to wu-wei, leaders try to make themselves obsolete, but remain available to those in need. This, to some extent, distinguishes Tao thinking from traditional Buddhism. Buddhism, according to Gary Snyder, has been willing to ignore politics and social action. Practitioners of Buddhism find peace by divorcing themselves from the social problems around them. They are not part of the problem, but neither are they an active part of the solution.[9] A Taoist philosophy does not afford the luxury of "dropping out," even when that choice would be very appealing. As Lin Yutang wrote, "The distinction between Buddhism and Taoism is this: the goal of the Buddhist is that he shall not want anything, while the goal of the Taoist is that he shall not be wanted at all. Only he who is not wanted by the public can be a carefree individual, and only he who is a carefree individual can be a happy human being."[10]

One reason that Taoist writing is interesting is its subtlety. A serious reader of the Tao must carefully work through the poetic prose, the metaphors, the stories, and the humor to discern the lessons. What Tao writing lacks in directness, however, it makes up for in redundancy. Instead of getting the reader's attention with a whack of the sledge, Tao writing tickles with a feather, once on the nose, then on the elbow, then on the feet – until finally the reader takes note and tries to find out what is causing the strange feeling.

The concept of not wanting to be needed, but serving when needed, is a good example of the Tao feather. It pops up so often in Tao writing that the reader slowly comes to the conclusion that it must be vitally important. The *Tao Te Ching* repeatedly encourages leaders and rulers to do nothing, but make sure everything gets done.[11] The *Wen-tzu* says that the effective leader succeeds without striving, yet acts when pressed and when there is no other choice.[12] The Tao writings of Lü Yan state that, "Even after you have attained nondoing, you should still carry out undertakings, fulfilling them and realizing their proper results."[13]

And as is often the case, the *Chuangtze* states the point as well as any of the Tao writings. On the subject of wu-wei, the classic work warns that while a philosophy of non-action is the only way to be one with the Tao, it also can entice people down the wrong path. Wu-wei can provide a leader with the personal balance from which to serve effectively and indiscreetly, but if he or she is not wary, it also can lead to idleness and a retirement from the world.[14]

From the perspective of not wanting to be needed, it may be reasonable to compare wu-wei leadership with laissez-faire leadership at its best. Neither has anything to do with being lazy. Neither has anything to do with not caring what direction the learning takes. Both, however, gently set the direction and the goals for the program, instill the students with a commitment to those directions and goals, and then leave a competent leader in the background, willing to step in only if needed.

Chapter 7 of the *Chuangtze* contrasts wu-wei leadership with a more authoritarian approach. The "mad man" Chieh Yü is asked about the style of leadership where the leader makes all the rules, sets all the standards, and determines all the methods. Chieh Yü responds:

> To try to govern the world like this is like trying to walk the ocean, to drill through a river, or to make a mosquito shoulder a mountain! When the sage governs, does he govern what is on the outside? He makes sure of himself first, and then he acts. He makes absolutely certain that things can do what they are supposed to do, that is all.[15]

WU-WEI IS NON-CONTRIVANCE.
While wu-wei usually is translated into English as non-ado, non-action, or do nothing, there is one significant exception. Thomas Cleary, perhaps the most prolific of the current translators of Taoist literature, uses the term "non-contrivance." For example, the common translation of Chapter 37 of the *Tao Te Ching* reads "The Tao does nothing, and yet nothing is left undone." The Cleary translation is "The Way is always uncontrived, yet there's nothing it doesn't do."[16] This careful wordage seems intentional. The term "non-contrivance" is too value laden to be used solely as a convenience. For Cleary, wu-wei connotes action that is real and necessary, not artificial, fabricated, or manipulated.

From an experiential education perspective, this is notable because much of what experiential educators set up for their students is contrived, even intentionally so.[17] Classroom experiences seldom are real, but are simulations of reality. Ropes course experiences are entirely contrived, conducted on telephone poles and aircraft cable and intended to symbolize the challenges and events of the real world. Both adventure therapy and experience-based training and development (EBTD) also include contrived activities that are supposed to generate metaphors that can be applied to real-life problems at work and in participants' personal lives. With perhaps the exception of service learning, internships, and backcountry travel, experiential education is contrived.

To me, a move toward non-contrivance is an interesting proposal. In the 1960s and early 1970s, alternative education (which was largely experiential) that was not contrived was criticized for a let's-go-do-something-and-see-what-happens attitude. The assumption of the method was that anything active was better than lecture and texts, so activity, in many instances, was done for activity's sake. There was no manipulation of the experience; what happened is what happened. The critics, however, saw it as kids gone wild and as play much more than education. The credibility of experiential education took a hit.

Ever since that time, experiential educators have been, through intentional contrivances, whittling away at directionlessness within their programming. Specific goals have been set, parameters on student freedom have been established and enforced, programs have been standardized, and debriefing has become as important as the experience itself. The result has been that much of the uncertainty has been taken out of experiential education, and there is much greater likelihood of consistent, predictable, and measurable outcomes. For the most part, these steps toward pre-determined outcomes have been taken without wondering whether something was being lost. There is a big difference between "Let's go into the wilderness and see what happens" and "Let's go into the wilderness and work on self-esteem." There is even a bigger difference between the "Let's go into the wilderness and see what happens" and "Let's go to the ropes course and work on self-esteem."

Maybe it is time to reflect back on whether the enhanced structure of experiential education is entirely a good thing. Obviously when a client or student has a specific goal in mind (e.g., addiction treatment, cooperation within the workplace), manipulating the experience to serve that need makes sense. Still, playfulness is a wonderful element of experiential education. Most grown-ups miss the playfulness that has slipped out of their lives as they have accepted the responsibilities of adulthood. Many children lose their love of learning as they enter the upper grades, where playfulness is wrung out of the curriculum. Play is spontaneous, flexible, unexpected, and free of disciplinary boundaries. Each manipulation by the educator to focus the purpose of a program toward a particular end cuts away at these fine attributes. Doing an activity for its own sake, as opposed to doing it for some predetermined purpose, is unusual in contemporary experiential education, and this is a loss.

Many years ago as a graduate student, I was dissatisfied with a Transcendental Meditation orientation because the only thing the presenters told me was that I would get better grades, make more money, have a more focused mind, and live longer if I practiced TM. Never once did they say that I would have fun meditating or that the meditative experience itself is a worthwhile pursuit. Sometimes I think that experiential education does the same thing as those TM presenters. A weekend canoe trip can be a tool to work on self-esteem, teamwork, physical health, stress reduction, and environmental awareness – but it also can be none of those things. The beauty of morning mist on the water, the joy of spotting a deer at the bend in the river, and the serenity of drifting on a gently flowing watercourse do not need to be assigned purposeful justifications. If anything, they are cheapened by such an attempt, and a weekend canoe trip can be nothing more than a float down the river.

WU-WEI COMES WITH MATURITY. IT TAKES TIME, WISDOM, AND EXPERIENCE.
As with most things, contrivance or non-contrivance is not an either/or matter. Both purposeful activity and activity for its own sake are valuable. Predetermined outcomes are good, but so are spontaneity and flexibility. A wu-wei response to the contrivance question would be that educators should contrive, but as little as is necessary.

Kenneth Boulding, in *The Image*, wrote that there are three ways that students may respond to teaching. The first is not at all, as information goes in one ear and out the other. The second is for students to take the information from teachers and use it to incrementally change their image of the world. For example, students can study the Czech Republic in school and slightly change their mental map of Europe. The third way, the most rare way, is for new information to totally change a student's image. Here a student undergoes a personal transformation, and from that point on, his or her perception of the world and his or her place in the world are altered.[18] The experience might be a major event, such as a death of a parent or a trip to a foreign country, but it might be no more than witnessing a particular piece of art or reading a special novel. For example, a student could visit Taliesan, Frank Lloyd Wright's home and school, and for the first time in her life see urban environments in terms of space and design.

My gut feeling is that the contriving of experiential education has clipped off both ends of Boulding's continuum. With predetermined outcomes, parameters, and standardization, there is less chance of experiential education affecting no change, but there is also less chance that life-altering change will occur. I compare it to a prepackaged vacation in a foreign land. The uncertainty has been winnowed away. The chances of being stranded, getting robbed, becoming sick have been minimized, but so have the chances of self-discovery, adventure, and trusting fate.

So with Boulding in mind, the experiential educators should consider weaning their students, but especially themselves, from contrived programming. This, however, comes only with experience as a leader. The novice naturalist relies on his pre-planned nature hike. The first-year teacher sticks closely to her lesson plans. The experienced naturalist or teacher, on the other hand, has her packaged program and predetermined outcomes, but does not necessarily abide by them. It is only with professional experience and maturity that an educator can stick to a planned program until something better comes along. It also is only with professional experience and maturity that an educator can start out with a let's-see-what-happens attitude, then smoothly shift to a pre-planned program if the spontaneous approach is not working. Finally it is only with experience and maturity that an educator can wait an experience out. While the novice educator usually is quick to jump into a problem and help make it right, the old timer sits on her hands/bites her tongue and steps in only after student frustration over the problem becomes, in Dewey's words, miseducation.[19]

Taoist writings say that wu-wei living and wu-wei leadership come only with experience. They come only with maturity or, as Alan Watts claimed, with a combination of wisdom and a history of taking the line of least resistance. As he wrote, "Wu-wei is thus the life-style of one who follows the Tao, and must be understood primarily as a form of intelligence – that is, of knowing the principles, structures, and trends of human and natural affairs so well that one uses the least amount of energy in dealing with them."[20]

Huang and Lynch echo Watts' sentiments, for they wrote, "Wu Wei movement comes with a certain level of experience; when we learn how smooth it feels to "blend" our efforts, Wu Wei becomes the obvious choice. Know that this takes time. Wu Wei, Wu Ji,* and other Tao concepts come naturally with experience, wisdom, and maturity."[21]


CONCLUSION

There is something intellectually exciting about coming across a word in one language that does not have an equivalent word in the person's native tongue. In some instances, it is an opportunity to learn about a concept that is entirely outside a person's current frame of thought. In other cases, it gives a name to an idea that has existed on the periphery of the person's thinking, but has yet to be named. Wu-wei is of this second type, and giving a name to a concept illuminates the lessons that can be derived from it. For example, I now recognize that valuing appropriate non-action in leadership is a manifestation of the Tao concept of wu-wei.

---

* Wu ji means emptiness and an open mind. Literally it translates as "no end."

Wu-wei and experiential education are not entirely compatible, and one reason for this incompatibility may be that Western thought has no clear place for this alien notion. It is an attribute that has not been considered. Having said this, however, there are a couple of lessons that can be derived from wu-wei. For example, a competent experiential educator helps only when needed. Another lesson is to contrive as little as possible. This means contrive when contrivance is the best reasonable alternative, not when it is merely the most convenient. An eight-hour ropes course program may be effective; a ten-day wilderness trip is likely to be even more effective. A game simulating homelessness and hunger makes a point; volunteering in a Salvation Army facility makes the point more emphatically. An addiction metaphor on a ropes course serves a purpose, but only as a complement to group or one-on-one counseling. Direct experience tends to be more effective than traditional classroom learning, and real experience tends to be more effective than contrived experience – but this does not mean that classroom learning and contrived experience are not useful.

I am tempted to say that the experience and maturity needed for wu-wei makes it a lofty standard for experiential education, something to strive for, even if never fully reached. This, however, would be poor advice. Striving for wu-wei would not be very wu-wei, and actively seeking wu-wei is not the way to find it. From wisdom, a joy for teaching, and a joy for spontaneity and going with the flow, wu-wei might result. If not, join the rest of us, for as the *Tao Te Ching* points out, "Unspoken guidance and uncontrived enhancement are reached by few in the world."[22]

MODERATION

# 4

# The Golden Carp

Clare was eating lunch by herself in the school cafeteria, and The Leader Who is Hardly Known asked if he could join her.

"Please do," she said. "I still feel strange eating in the cafeteria alone, and this'll give me a chance to thank you for helping me through the semester. It made a big, big difference."

"You're welcome," said the Leader Who is Hardly Known. "It's been a long time, but I can still remember my first teaching assignment. I am happy that I could help. And congratulations. You're nearly through your first semester, and you still have a smile on your face."

Clare's usual smile grew even bigger at the comment, and she said, "It hasn't been easy. I feel like all that I have done the past three months is work. I must have learned a lot, but I've been so overwhelmed that I haven't stopped to figure out what that learning might be. After I've graded finals and turned in grades, I'll have to take the time to think back on the last few months."

"Don't rush it. For me, it took a couple of years of teaching before I felt comfortable enough to not worry about the day-to-day and to start thinking about philosophies and other big-picture considerations. It would be wonderful to have a grand vision of teaching before you ever start teaching, but in my experience, it doesn't work that way. Hard to worry about theory when you don't even know where to get a new bulb for the overhead projector."

"More good advice," said Clare. "And as long as you are dispensing it, I have a question for you. It's something that's been on my mind ever since I held a couple of review sessions for final exams. How do you respond when students blatantly ask you what they need to know for the test?"

"Ah," said the Leader Who is Hardly Known. "You want the students to care about learning, and all they want to know is what's on the test."

"I guess. I don't blame students for wanting good grades. We've all been trained to go after grades. But I care about the subject matter so much, and I sure don't see my enthusiasm rubbing off on anyone as exam time comes along."

"Instead students are asking you what's the least they need to know to get through the semester?"

"Yeah," responded Clare. "That's what bugs me. The students don't want to learn as much as possible. They want to learn as little as possible."

"I disagree a little bit with the way you put it," said the Leader Who is Hardly Known. "Not as little as possible, but as little as necessary. There's a difference. It's like a computer expert taking an hour to show you all the fancy stuff that a new word processing program can do, when you only wanted her to show you how to make mailing labels. All that other stuff is interesting, but right then you only care about mailing your packages."

"So you take the students' side in working for the grade."

"No," said the Leader Who is Hardly Known, "but I do think that the students' question makes sense. For a teacher, knowing more about a subject is good. It affords flexibility in teaching. It digs a deeper well to draw from. For a student though, I don't think that it is always good to know as much as possible about any one subject. With so much to learn and so much to do, a student asking what is the least that he needs to know at this point in his life, so he can move on to other things, seems a reasonable question.[1] Look at a normal curriculum today. The three R's get their time slots, and then environmental education, physical education, information technology, music, art, foreign language, and a half dozen other valuable subjects and skills all vie for the remaining limited space. If teachers did a better job of figuring out the essentials in their particular field, students might have time for a broader education and actually learn more than they do now. Teachers could, of course, mentor the few students who develop a passion for a particular subject, but why jam all students with as much information as possible? Treat them as you would the golden carp."

"The gold carp? I knew that you would work this around to one of your Chinese legends," joked Clare.

"Is it my fault that the problems we face today have troubled humankind for thousands of years? I do, in fact, have an ancient Chinese story that sheds light on the subject at hand, and if I was eating lunch with someone who valued the wisdom of the ages, I might be persuaded to tell it."

Clare set down her sandwich so that she could mimic a kowtow. "Oh please wise master! Please bless this ignorant soul with the story of some ol' yellow fish."

The Leader Who is Hardly Known responded, "With such sarcasm, I am tempted to not tell you and leave you wondering. Lucky for you, I like to tell stories, and this story is of Chuangtze when he was down on his luck. His family was without food, so he went to the marquis to borrow some grain. The marquis was a man of good intentions, so he said, 'The tax money will come soon, and then I can lend you three hundred pieces of gold. How will that be?'"

"Chuangtze looked at the marquis as if he had lost his mind and then responded, 'Yesterday, on my way to see you, I heard a voice coming from the middle of the road. I looked down, and there was a golden carp lying in the carriage rut. I said, "Golden carp, what are you doing here?"

"'The fish replied, "I am the minister of the waves of the Eastern Sea. Could you give me a dipperful of water to keep me alive?"

"'I told the carp, "Yes, I am heading south and will soon meet the West River. I can channel water from the river to come meet you. How will that be?"

"'The golden carp became angry and said, "Don't you understand? Look at me! I'm lost. I am way out of my element. I have no place to go. If you give me a dipper of water, I might stay alive. If you offer to help me by rerouting rivers, just come back and find me in a dried fish shop.""[2]

# GOOD ENOUGH IS GOOD ENOUGH

> *If we irrigate during the rainy season, aren't we exercising poor management.*[3]
>
> Chuangtze

There are a couple of things about wu-wei that did not get discussed in the previous chapter. One common sense observation is that if wu-wei means accomplishing the task with as little energy as is necessary, then leading in a way that is consistent with wu-wei is, whenever possible, preventive rather than reactive. It is dealing with problems while they are still small. Better still, it is setting people on the right track from the start and avoiding the need to intervene later on. As Lao-tzu stated it:

> *Plan for difficulty when it is still easy, do the great while it is still small. The most difficult things in the world must be done while they are easy; the greatest things in the world must be done while they are small.*[4]

There are two points worth mentioning concerning preventative action, and both deal with not taking it to extremes. The first is the importance of knowing when to step in and when to step back (i.e., let the group work the problem out). A leader wants to take action to avoid big problems, but not jump in every time a group hits a bump. The trick is discerning what small problems are the early stages of something beyond the group's capabilities.

The second point about preventative action is to not become obsessive about it. The objective of prevention management is to take small steps early to avoid big problems later; it is not to consider every eventuality, no matter how small, then spend more time and effort avoiding a potential problem than it would take to address the problem if it occurred. For example, it is a good idea to prepare for a backpacking trip, but it is not a good idea to let over-preparation sap all the fun out of the trip. It is a good idea to pack for the unexpected in the backcountry, but it is a bad idea to pack a hundred pounds of gear so that you are ready for every possible medical emergency, every possible equipment malfunction, and every weather condition that the particular wilderness area has ever had. As Thoreau put it, "We are determined to be starved before we are hungry. Men say that a stitch in time saves nine, and so they take a thousand stitches to-day to save nine tomorrow."[5]

## MODERATION IS GOOD ENOUGH

A second aspect of leading or teaching according to wu-wei that was not mentioned in the previous chapter, and is the primary topic of this chapter, is the concept of "good enough." Part of unnecessarily turning a small thing into a big thing is reworking and reworking a project for incremental improvements. While all of us are familiar with examples of shoddiness and lackadaisical effort, I would say that we can think of just as many instances where a person has nitpicked for perfection when good enough is good enough, maybe even when good enough is preferable to perfection. For example, people maintain perfect lawns by spending hundreds of dollars on gadgets and many hours in direct contact with herbicides and fertilizers. Others pump iron for perfect bodies, when, in fact, maximum health would be something less extreme. While I will never be accused of having an immaculate lawn or a perfect physique, the concept of good enough strikes home as I write this book. For the last six weeks I have been toiling with this particular chapter, in effect trying to make perfect a short essay that is about not being perfect. I spend an hour or more on each paragraph, and I actually lie in bed at night running various arrangements of words through my head. Should I be satisfied with "good enough," set my writing aside, and spend more time playing with my three-year old daughter? I honestly can't decide, for I do want the book to be as good as my writing skills will allow. Also I know what my daughter would say.

For those raised on striving for excellence, on giving a hundred percent, on always doing their best, on doing well at anything worth doing, wu-wei asks that they consider easing back on the need for perfection. Or as Chuangtze stated it, "The sun and moon are out, and yet the torches remain burning. Doesn't too much light just make things all the more difficult?"[6] Lao tzu said the same thing, but of course, in fewer words, when he wrote, "When you have done your work, retire!"[7]

Lin Yu-tang observed that the obsession for perfection is a Western, especially an American, phenomenon. He wrote:

> The desire for one hundred per cent efficiency seems almost obscene. The trouble with Americans is that when a thing is nearly right, they want to make it better, while for a Chinese, nearly right is good enough.... One must start out with a belief that there are no catastrophes in this world, and besides the noble art of getting things done, there is a nobler art of leaving things undone.[8]

## GOOD ENOUGH AND EXPERIENTIAL EDUCATION

So, for experiential education, what is good enough? The answer to this question very much depends upon the educational setting. Those who work in the traditional classroom may be forced to identify exactly the point of good enough, because such a determination has real life consequences for students. I am not talking about the inconsequential distinction between an A- and a B+, but the difference between passing or not passing a course, the difference between graduating or not graduating to the next grade level.

Unfortunately the Tao does not have much good advice on this tough situation, except perhaps to question the need to grade at all. In my own job at a university, I have to grade students and find it one of the most distasteful parts of teaching. I will say, however, that in my courses that are extensively experiential, the need to give a failing grade is rare.

Fortunately most experiential educators (i.e., those outside of the traditional classroom) are not handcuffed with letter grades or pro- motion decisions, so they can look at the notion of good enough in a more casual way. For example, they can be more concerned with level of engagement and less about level of performance. They can support and facilitate solid performance, but not to the point of causing burn out or stress. As with so much involving the Tao, moderation is the key – and with moderation, comes some fuzziness. There is no need to establish an exact measure of good enough, because such exactness serves no purpose.

The most valuable part of doing away with external measures such as grading, however, is not the burden lifted from the shoulders of the teachers; it is the newfound freedom available to the students. They no longer need to please teachers or reach a set standard, but can turn to self-determined goals and levels of performance. This shift changes the role of the educator significantly. The task of the teacher then is not to look at each activity and determine what level of effort is good enough; instead it is the loftier goal of helping students develop an intelligent approach in discerning for themselves those tasks that deserve a commitment for excellence and those that do not. Freedom in an educational setting is novel for most students, so they often lack tools to determine what is good enough and what is not. They might not have the maturity to know what deserves a best effort and what does not. The job of the educator, therefore, moves from setting standards for students to helping students set standards for themselves. This is a fairly excit- ing concept, for instead of centering on short-term goals, it is devel- oping a tool for lifelong learning. Two suggestions for helping students develop their own sense of good enough are as follows:

## 1. Provide challenges where the measure of good enough is obvious to all.

One way to help students determine a sense of good enough is to give them tasks where the measure of good enough is self-evident. Another way to state this is to provide tasks that do not need an external standard of measure (i.e., no letter grade, no national average, no score from a panel of judges). The task is performed either well enough or not well enough, and the person performing the task knows immediately the difference. This is not so much in reference to competitive activities where the measure of success is bettering a less skilled opponent, but to tasks where the measure of success is whether the results work. For example, if I am trying to get over a creek by crossing on a fallen log, it is good enough if I get across; it is not good enough if I slip and fall in the creek. It makes no difference whether my friend scampered across like a squirrel and I crawled over on my hands and knees. If I reached my destination safely and stayed dry, that's good enough.

Experiential education is replete with activities where the realization of good enough is easy to see. A paddler on a river either glides through a narrow chute or gets the canoe hung up on a rock. An orienteerer either takes a correct bearing or ends up in the wrong place. The feedback in these cases is immediate and apparent, the antithesis of waiting for a judge or a teacher to determine whether the performance passed muster.

In *Shouting at the Sky*, the popular book about troubled youth at a Utah-based wilderness program, much is made of building camp-fires with the use of a bow and drill. While a purist would rightly point out that there are standards for fire building (e.g., smokiness, minimum impact, fire safety), the measure of success basically is whether there is a fire. Fire building is a very practical example of good enough. Even when a student's matches are taken away and replaced by more primitive fire starting tools such as a bow and drill, it still remains almost pointless to compare one person's fire to another's. There is no national standard for which to judge campfires, and no one will be getting into Harvard for making an unusually good bed of coals for cooking (even if it is a talent deserving of respect). Even if a leader brought together a group of students to evaluate a fire building exercise, the true measure of "good enough" would be whether the group had a warm fire to sit around while they carried on the conversation.

Many group initiatives on a ropes and challenge course have self-evident measures of good enough. This is demonstrated by the spontaneous cheering and clapping that frequently erupts from a group at the instant that they complete the last component of a difficult task. Still, in spite of the excitement surrounding the success, a common question from participants following the initiative is, "Well, how did other groups do this?" The common and appropriate response from the facilitator is to avoid a straightforward answer. Instead he or she will say something like, "It doesn't matter how other groups have done it," or "I don't like to compare groups. Today is your experience and only your experience," or more provocatively, "Good enough is good enough. Why does it matter how another group did it?"

## 2. LEAD STUDENTS TO ACTIVITIES THAT ARE INTRINSICALLY MOTIVATING.

Unfortunately many tasks are not so clean cut that the measure of good enough is obvious. Whereas everyone can say with certainty that one stack of wood is a campfire and another stack is a failed attempt at a campfire, measuring good enough in such things as art, music, and physical activity is much more subjective. It is not even the end product that needs to be judged good enough, because a very good experience could result in a product that is lousy. All of us have done things where the finished product goes immediately to the junk heap, but still the experience was enjoyable and satisfying. Chesterton wrote that "anything worth doing is worth doing poorly,"[9] which, if you think about it, makes as much sense as the more traditional form of the proverb.

Perhaps for tasks that have an unclear measure of good enough, the gauge should be the participant's level of engagement during the activity. In other words, how much is the person into it? In the ideal, all of us should be more mindful of just about everything that we do; this applies even for simple actions such as eating an orange, washing the dishes, or riding a bicycle. However, a taken-for-granted part of contemporary life is to do two or three things simultaneously. People want to accomplish more within a finite period of time, so they either take on more than one task at a time or substitute a slow activity with something that can be done more quickly (fast food, cell phones, shorter vacations, etc.). Robinson and Godbey call this trend "time deepening,"[10] but it really is time shallowing, for as more activities are crammed into a day, each of them is getting done at a more shallow or superficial level.

In a convoluted sense, a person might interpret multitasking as part of the Tao concept of good enough. It certainly is choosing mediocre results over perfection; nothing is done well when a person's concentration is spread over two or more things at the same time. Conversely, a person who has freed himself from an obsession with perfection has not gained much if the newfound freedom just gets sucked into a black hole of countless other tasks. As inexact as the Tao concept of good enough is, I am sure that it does not include doing unimportant things quickly in order to free up time to do other unimportant things just as quickly. A primary characteristic of Tao activity is "the loss of awareness of the passage of time,"[11] whereas a hallmark of multitasking is just the opposite, a constant eye on the clock.

Therefore, a second way that an experiential educator can train people to develop their own sense of good enough is to help students find happiness by doing the things that are important to them – doing them without fear of not being good enough – doing them without concern for how long it takes. Of course when a student takes on an entirely new activity, there are basic skills to be taught that are not necessarily intrinsically interesting, but after these basics are understood by students, education should turn those students loose to find and fill their own niche. As the ancient *Huainanzi* puts it, "Place a monkey in a cage, and it is the same as a pig, not because it isn't clever and quick, but because it has no place to freely exercise its capabilities."[12]

With this freer approach to education, learning would be much more of a hobby than it is now. I use the word "hobby" in a positive sense, because one of the most admirable things that a person can be is a serious amateur.[13]  If I use my own late father as an example, I do not think of him as an employee of the gas and electric company or as the guy who fell asleep in front of the television.  He is the man who taught me to trout fish and who carved the intricate duck decoys that now fill a display case in my living room.  Perhaps with the exception of his family, my dad's hobbies are what most defined him as a person.

The ancient Greek word for leisure is "scholé," from which come the English words "school" and "scholar."  Scholé means performance of activity for its own sake or as its own end.[14]  With scholé in mind, a task of quality education is to help students figure out what activities intrinsically motivate them and then to create an atmosphere where these activities can be performed not for a grade or other form of external approval, but for their own sake.

Psychologist Mihalyi Csikszentmihalyi calls these intrinsically satisfying actions flow activities, activities that so engage the participant that she becomes part of the action and temporarily loses a sense of time.  Whether it is paddling a kayak, playing an instrument, or solving a mathematical problem, Csikszentmihalyi claims that flow activities have three common features.  They have 1) a clear objective, 2) immediate feedback as to how the person did, and 3) a level of difficulty that matches the skill level of the person who is engaged in the activity (i.e., is neither too easy, nor too difficult).  In a flow activity, the individual is challenged, but so in control of the situation she knows she is up to the task.[15]

Csikszentmihalyi goes on to point out that there are people who consciously try to fill their lives with flow experiences.  He credits these people with having what he calls an autotelic personality and suggests that traditional education incorrectly sucks this positive attribute out of people.  He concludes by saying that great thinkers since Plato have recognized experiential education as the promoter of the autotelic personality, but that traditional education tends to ignore "training of the whole person, building on spontaneous interests and potentialities..., while making possible a joyous experience of growth."[16]

It may be unrealistic to think that educators can discern which activities intrinsically motivate each of their students and then regularly provide these activities at levels of difficulty that demand full engagement. Most people cannot even do that for themselves. However, it seems that educators can lay groundwork to help students foster an autotelic personality. To do so, in my mind, would be good enough. At the beginning of this chapter, I suggested that part of wu-wei was preventative action; in other words, set the stage and get out of the way. Good education is preventative action. If students at a young age had been encouraged to pursue their hearts' desires, would there be as much low self-esteem, as much mid-life crisis, as much need for antisocial cheap thrills to fill the voids in people's lives? In other words, would we all be happier and healthier had education taught us to follow our bliss?

## CONCLUSION

If the term humorist is defined as a person who makes fun of the shortcomings of one's own culture, then working too hard to achieve perfection must be a shortcoming of modern Western (or maybe English speaking) society. I've already mentioned Chesterton's "anything worth doing is worth doing poorly" quote, but there are several others with the same sentiment. Mark Twain, for example, said, "Do not put off until tomorrow what can be put off till day-after-tomorrow just as well."[17] Thurber mirrored Twain by stating, "Early to rise and early to bed makes a male healthy and wealthy and dead."[18] Will Rogers said, "If you find yourself in a hole, the first thing to do is stop diggin'."[19] And while Maughn hardly falls into the category of humorist, he added his own perspective on the subject by writing, "Perfection has one grave defect; it is apt to be dull."[20]

No one has a definitive answer to the question of what is good enough. Maybe the best that can be done is to be cognizant that moderation is not limited to material goods, but includes the expenditure of energy.[21] For me, this awareness sometimes makes me question myself midway through activities, even some that I have been doing for years. For example, I was literally stopped in my tracks while exercising during a recent trip to Hong Kong. Running on a paved pathway halfway up Victoria Peak, I realized that the only jogger on the entire route was me, even though I was passing dozens of elderly Chinese who were doing their dzao tao or morning exercises. A few were going through tai chi routines, some were walking with friends, but most were just twisting their torsos and shaking their arms. Even though I intellectually knew that jogging was hard on my knees, it was the first time that I ever thought running might be pushing my body too hard. My jogging pace is barely faster than a quick walk, but there still is a dramatic contrast between the joint-jarring pounding of my run and the gentle movements these Chinese elders use to loosen muscles and move blood. As a result of the experience, I no longer jog. Instead of running for thirty minutes, I now walk for an hour; and even though this adds a half hour to my workout, it might help me to live as long as many of the people whom I saw on Victoria Peak. If so, great. If not, a solo walk is more mindful than a run, and that, I have decided, is good enough.

STEADINESS

# 5

# The Runaway Horse

Nancy, the waterfront director, sat on the front step of her cabin looking pensive. The Leader Who is Hardly Known walked up and sat along side her on the stoop. "Bothered or just thinking?" he asked.

The director looked over at the Leader Who is Hardly Known and said, "Mostly thinking, I guess. Today the waterfront staff did compliment cards. Do you know what they are?"

"No, I never heard of them."

"Compliment cards are when everyone on a staff takes a stack of three-by-five cards and writes a compliment about every other person on the staff. Someone collects the cards, sorts them by the recipient of the compliment, and then everyone has a pile of compliments about themselves. The purpose is to help get the group through the mid-season slump by showing them that they are appreciated."

"Sounds like they could be helpful to some people."

"Yeah, but I've been reading my cards, and they are all the same. They say I'm steady. I'm dependable. I'm reliable. I'm consistent. The comments were all meant to be complimentary, but I can't help but think that it's not the stuff that motivates a staff."

"It is what holds a staff together when difficulties come up," said the Leader Who is Hardly Known. "I think of myself as a good leader, but I have never been dynamic. I don't even consider myself enthusiastic."

"Yeah, but there is something about you that appeals to people," said Nancy. "Once they know you, they respect you. But it's more than steadiness. It is something else. It's a calmness."

"Thank you. I take that as a compliment, but I won't let it go to my head. Part of a calm disposition is not letting compliments, or criticisms for that matter, affect me too much. In fact, it reminds me of one of the great stories of Tao literature. Have I ever told you the story of the Runaway Horse?"

"No, I don't think so."

"Ah well, let me tell you. It might shed some light on your concern with the dullness of being steady. There once was a farmer whose horse ran away. All those around him bemoaned the loss, but the farmer remained steady, even if the absence of the horse meant harder work for him. A week later the horse returned, bringing four wild horses with him. All those around him rejoiced at the farmer's good fortune, but the farmer kept an even keel, even if the horses, when broken, would bring him welcome income. Then one day, while his son was breaking one of the new horses, the horse bucked, and the son fell and broke his leg. All those around him expressed sorrow at the son's pain and the farmer's loss of a worker, but the farmer accepted the accident as the natural course of things. The very next day, the army came through the farmer's village, taking all young men off to war. The farmer's son was excused, because he had a broken leg. All the people said that the farmer was very lucky to keep his son, but the farmer's heart remained calm throughout.[1]

"That's the whole story. While all those around the farmer moved from extreme happiness to extreme sadness and back again, the farmer knew that life was too complex to be explained by any single event. His goal was to keep a light heart, regardless of the events beyond his control."

"So," asked Nancy, "I should be glad that my staff thinks I am steady?"

"No, you're not listening," answered the Leader Who is Hardly Known. "Steadiness means being neither glad nor sad over what your staff wrote on their compliment cards. I know that it is hard not to care what others think of you, but if this relatively small thing is really bothering you, then you may not be as steady as they think. Look at what has just happened. Something that was intended to boost your spirits has had the opposite effect. Not only that, but those bad feelings have clouded your ability to learn from the experience. What have you just learned?"

"I've learned that compliment cards have the power to hurt. If they've made me feel a little bit bad, then they could have had the same effect on some of my staff."

"Now that is thinking like a leader. A big part of leadership is not to be knotted up about yourself, so your mind and heart are free to learn about those under your guidance."

"I just thought of something else," said Nancy. "The staff was telling me what they appreciate in a supervisor. If I look at the cards as a lesson in leadership rather than a reflection on me, I can see that people want to work under someone who is steady."

 CALM STEADINESS

> *If you are disturbed by bee stings and distracted by mosquito bites, how do you think you can be calm and empty in the face of the troubles that oppress the human mind, which are more serious than the venom of a bee sting and the annoyance of mosquito bites?*[2]
>
> Huainanzi

Tao thinking values calm steadiness as a character trait. Its writings frequently mention keeping a consistent attitude under all conditions. A person whose emotions fluctuate with every small shift of events is hardly someone who can remain calm during the constant variation of daily life. The most famous example of steadiness in Tao writing is the runaway horse story mentioned in the fable that opened this chapter. Other quotes expressing the same sentiment include:

> From the *Huainanzi*, "Calamity and fortune will not be able to disturb you, censure and praise will not be able to affect you. Therefore you can reach the ultimate."[3]

> From the *Tao Te Ching*, "He who adheres assiduously to the path of Tao is a man of steady purpose."[4]

> From *Sayings of Ancestor Lü*, "To learn the Way we first kill off the chief hoodlum. What is the chief hoodlum? It is emotions."[5]

> From *Secret Records of Understanding the Way* "I always tell people that the first essential of practice is to even the temper well."[6]

> From the *Wentzu*, which repeatedly addresses this theme, "Though people may be of the east, west, south, or north, you stand alone in the middle."[7]

> Also from the *Wentzu*, "Nothing pleases them, nothing pains them, nothing delights them, nothing angers them. All things are mysteriously the same; there is neither right nor wrong."[8]

> Again from the *Wentzu*, "When (sages) are happy they are not overjoyed, and when they grieve they are not hopelessly distressed. Thus they are not in danger even in high places; they are secure and stable."[9]

> And still again from the *Wentzu*, "Sadness and happiness are deviations of virtue, likes and dislikes are a burden to the mind, joy and anger are excesses on the way."[10]

## STEADINESS RECONSIDERED

The frequent references to steadiness in the Tao literature were so pervasive that they actually caused me to reconsider my view on the character trait, and in doing so I discovered a flaw in my thinking. When I asked myself to come up with words that describe an experiential educator, enthusiastic immediately came to mind, as did dynamic, motivational, and adventurous. At the mention of adventurous, however, I realized that these were characteristics that I *associated* with experiential educators; they were not necessarily terms that I most *valued* in experiential educators. In a person responsible for the well-being of others, adventurous was a trait that struck me as too daring. Although many good experiential educators are adventurous in their personal lives, what I valued in their leadership was an ability to tone down their own affinity for risk when exposing others to potentially risky activities. I realized that I wanted experiential educators who were a bit more steady.

Because my first description of an experiential educator did not get at the question I was trying to answer, I then tried a slightly different approach. I reworded the initial question and asked myself to list the characteristics that I most wanted in an experiential educator who was also my co-worker. When I added this qualifier to the question, the results were different. Enthusiasm no longer headed the list, and adventurous did not even come to mind. Honesty, fairness, openness, commitment, knowledge, reliability, and steadiness all struck me as more important than enthusiasm. Zeal for the work, of course, was important, but above all else, I wanted co-workers who could be trusted to do their jobs well.

What explained this difference? Did I really value enthusiasm when speaking hypothetically, but then value something completely different when getting down to brass tacks and talking about the person I had to work alongside? The answer, I'm afraid, was "yes." The reason, however, was not that I was hypocritical or intentionally dishonest with myself. It was more that I had not thought much about this issue before, and the inconsistencies between the hypothetical and the actual had gone unnoticed. Now that reading the Tao had me thinking about personality traits in a more serious way, it was perhaps inevitable that some of my earlier thoughts would not make sense. One of the weakly held beliefs to quickly fall was that I valued gung ho enthusiasm over steadiness.

One reason for this misreading was that I had a false assumption about the meaning of steadiness. Steady does not necessarily mean deadpan, nor does it mean stern. It means consistent and unflappable, so a person can be both steady and spirited. Liu I-ming called it being both round and square. He wrote, "The round cannot remain stationary, the square cannot roll around – each has its own nature.... When you can be round and square, following the rules of the compass and square, then you do not fall into stagnant fixation or random suggestibility. Outwardly you are lively and active, inwardly you are calm and sure."[11]

When I actually think about the very best people I have worked with, I realize that I would not actually describe them as enthusiastic. That is too strong a term. These people were lighthearted, but they were not educational cheerleaders. The best evidence of this was that there was not a significant change in personality when they dropped whatever they were doing and went to work with students. When I teach leadership in my university courses, I talk about developing a persona. Persona, in this case, is not creating a false personality, but is putting a best face forward when going before a group; it is temporarily putting personal aggravations aside and giving full attention to the task at hand. When I think of the best experiential educators, however, there was not much change when shifting into work mode. Because these people were upbeat before they started a class, there was no need to turn on the switch when teaching. I am not saying that they were inhumanly oblivious to the annoyances of life, but their normal countenance was an ongoing quiet cheerfulness. It made me want to be around them, and it made them excellent educators.

This upbeat personality is consistent with the Tao concept of calm steadiness. Steady does not mean stoic. Well, it could mean stoic, because stoic in the classic sense need not mean glum and stone faced. The Greek Stoics, contrary to the humorless connotation often associated with their philosophy, were more about steadiness than they were sternness. In fact, they, as much as Plato, Aristotle, and the Epicureans, were seeking a path to happiness. For the Stoics, happiness was achieved by not letting the inevitable occurrence of bad things compromise their sense of right thought and right action. The Stoics believed that a good life came with accepting those things that were beyond a person's control and committing oneself to improving those things where a person could make a difference.[12]

From this viewpoint, the Stoics have much in common with the Tao. Calm steadiness is maintaining a gently cheerful demeanor under all conditions. As the *Huainanzi* stated it, "Take the world lightly, and your spirit will not be burdened... Great people are serene, free from longing; they are calm, free from worry."[13] The Tao accepts change as a given, and steadiness is maintaining the same frame of mind regardless of the direction those changes take. Steadiness does not mean revealing no emotion. It means being consistently lighthearted – taking things seriously, but never so seriously that it squashes a slightly comic frame of mind. One of the reasons that *Chuangtze* is a bit difficult to read is that it often has a comic edge to it, and the reader is left wondering whether the author is being serious or satirical. Lin Yutang actually tells us to "read (Chuangtze) as one would a humorist writer, knowing that he is frivolous when he is profound and profound when he is frivolous."[14]

## A Calm and Steady Educator

When I think of calm steadiness, I sometimes envision a peaceful monk with a hint of a smile on the corners of his mouth. This Buddha-like character is carefree and fully content at what he is doing at that moment. Unfortunately for the educator in me, the monk in this mental image is wearing saffron robes and living on the grounds of a Thai temple. I cannot just take this monastic example and apply it directly to experiential education theory. Still I have seen that same subtle smile on topnotch experiential educators in the course of their work. It creeps onto their faces when they observe a student who is "getting it." It shows up when they take a group to a natural area of exceptional serenity. Actually I have seen it most often on canoe trips, when a leader casually paddling momentarily loses herself in the rhythmic patterns of the river. The canoe stroke becomes as meditative as sitting in a lotus position, and the experiential educator, for a time, does take on the leisurely countenance of a Thai monk.

Calm steadiness becomes increasingly important the longer that an educator is in contact with a particular group of students. In a two-hour lecture, for example, an audience may enjoy and learn a great deal from someone who is brilliant, but unstable. That does not necessarily make him a good teacher and certainly does not make him a good experiential educator. Experiential education, even more than a lecture form of teaching, requires extreme stability because students need to know how their leader will react at all times. It is not realistic to expect students to take creative chances, to make mistakes, to be experiential, if they are on constant alert as to how their actions will affect the mood of the leader. As Huang and Lynch stated it, "We must be consistent in our approaches and ways of being, and avoid erratic behavior that would create insecurity, tension, and fear."[15]

Once educators come to value steadiness, they take small steps to remain steady in their leadership. First of all, they slow down and put less pressure upon themselves. The trend in experiential education may be to accomplish more in less time, but this creates rushed programs and somewhat manic programmers. Diminished opportunities for mentorship aside, intensely compacted curricula mean leaders cannot perform well program after program. It asks for a pace that is not sustainable.

In addition to slowing down, leaders help themselves out by having realistic expectations of how much good they can accomplish. Educators rarely make immediate significant changes, so it makes no sense to judge on this basis. According to Lin Yutang's interpretation of Tao thinking, "An educated man is one who believes he has not succeeded when he has, but is not so sure he has failed when he fails, while the mark of the half-educated man is his assumptions that his outward successes and failures are absolute and real."[16]

Self-evaluation is worthwhile, but frequent self-criticism, especially criticism for being imperfect, serves no useful purpose.

According to the Tao, a person actually performs better once the stakes of the performance are lessened. In other words, a teacher is more effective once she realizes that she doesn't have to change the world. The *Lieh-tzu* compared it to the difference between playing a game for fun and playing it on a bet. The game for fun is more spontaneous, more creative, and better played. "If it's your money that's at stake, you'll fumble. It's not that you've lost your skill. It's because you are so flustered by things happening outside that you've lost your calmness inside. Lose your stillness and you will fail in everything you do."[17] Coincidently, this applies to students as well as teachers. For example, studies have shown that elementary school students create better art projects when they know that the project is not going to be judged. As soon as the assignment becomes a competition or a graded assignment, the artwork loses the playfulness and creativity that make it good.[18]

## CONCLUDING ANECDOTE

When I was in graduate school in the 1980's, I was a teaching assistant responsible for teaching one or two undergraduate courses each semester. While I had taught environmental education for many years before pursuing an advanced degree, the assistantship was my first classroom teaching, and I did not feel that I was making a good transition from the field to the classroom. When I brought up my concerns to a group of graduate students and full-time instructors, one professor responded to my self-criticism by saying, "Don't feel too bad about your bad classes, and don't feel too good about your good classes. You might be the only one who can tell the difference."[19]

At the time of the discussion, I took the statement to be advice about steadiness; don't be too hard on myself, don't expect too much from my courses, certainly look at the big picture and don't worry about one or two classes that flop. About a week later, I realized that I had misinterpreted the somewhat cryptic suggestion.

The professor was not telling me not to be so hard on myself. He was telling me to find some humility. I should not think so highly of myself that I'd assume anybody was paying any attention to my minor goof-ups in the classroom. The students in my classes hardly noticed, and nobody else even knew or cared what was happening.

Today, about twenty years later, I have reinterpreted the statement a third time and now think that it is about both steadiness and humility. I am not sure that the professor even knew the depth of his statement; he may have, as he was a man of unusual depth. I am sure that he did not realize that the statement would stick with me for two decades and help me realize that steadiness and humility go hand in hand. If I am humble and understand the insignificance of my thoughts and actions, then I will not take myself so seriously. Once that happens, lighthearted steadiness will follow.

# SECTION TWO
## Teaching Tips

gentle push

Tao literature does not offer many overt specifics about education programming. There are several contemporary books with titles such as *The Tao of Teaching*, *The Tao of Learning*, and *Teaching in the Tao*,[1] but they are like this book in that they identify Tao concepts about ruling a country and/or living a full life and then tweak them to fit the issues of the education profession. The next four chapters are fairly generic Tao concepts that do have direct application to the field of education. The four are 1) the aftermath of challenge, 2) the yin and the yang, 3) the distinctions between a leader and a manager, and 4) the importance of teaching only when the student is ready for the content.

yin/yang

Leadership

appropriate
timing

GENTLE PUSH

# 6

# The Boy Who Stepped on a Bee

Mary, the camp naturalist was just turning off the lights and closing the door of the nature center when the Leader Who is Hardly Known walked by. "Mary, how was your day today?" he asked.

Mary grimaced a bit, which was not her usual response. "Fine," she said, "if you consider lying to a kid acceptable behavior."

"Well, it's not acceptable, but I'm sure you're exaggerating," responded the Leader Who is Hardly Known.

"No, I lied. A big fat, in the kid's face, lie. And if that isn't enough, it's the second time in a row that I lied to the same kid. My intentions were good, but I still feel lousy. I think I may have hurt the kid's feelings, which is exactly what I was trying to avoid in the first place.

"The real goof up was two weeks ago," Mary continued. "I was sitting with a group of kids, and we were passing around a beaver tail and a woodpecker skull and some other stuff that I use to teach animal adaptation. As I am passing the animal parts around, a bee starts buzzing around one girl. The girl freaks out, so Dwight, this great little kid, jumps up and tries to kill the bee. Instinctively I shout out 'don't hurt the bee,' but I say it just as Dwight's shoe comes right down on the bee and squashes it flat. It actually was a pretty athletic move, because he swatted the bee out of the air with the sole of his shoe, then drove it to the ground and smashed it underfoot.

"The look on Dwight's face broke my heart. He had been in camp all week, he loved nature, so he'd been around me a lot – and now he disappointed me because he'd killed one of nature's creatures after I told him not to. The expression on his face looked like he'd run over my dog. The poor kid was trying to help the freaked out girl, and in the process, he ended up doing what he thought was a bad thing. I knew that just telling him that it was okay would not relieve his pain, so I immediately tried to comfort him by saying, "Here's a problem we have to solve. Personally I don't think it is wrong to kill nature. Humans have to kill plants and animals to have food and shelter. What bothers me is killing nature for no worthwhile reason. In fact, I have a rule that anything I kill I have to use. Dwight just did a good thing. He helped Trish, who was afraid of bees, but in helping her, he killed a bee. The problem now is figuring out how we can use a dead bee. One possible solution is to eat it. Is anybody willing to help us out and eat the bee? No takers? Well then we have to figure out something else.

"Dwight's face immediately relaxed, and it was actually Dwight who suggested that we use the wings and the legs from the bee to make slides for the stereoscopes in the nature center. I said that that was a good idea, but that it was dinner time, so I would have to make the slides another day. I stuck the bee in my pocket.

"It was the second to the last day of the session, the kids went home, and I forgot about the bee. A week later I found it in my jacket pocket, and I threw it in the trash. This week, however, little Dwight came back. He had such a great time at camp, his parents signed him up for another week. This morning he comes flying into the nature center, all excited about seeing the bee slides. Of course, there were no slides, so I lied to him. I told him that the bee was so smashed that the wings and the legs didn't work for slides. I lied when I said that I would make slides, and now I'm covering my ass with lies on top of lies. Again the little guy looked crushed, so this afternoon he and I went out with a butterfly net and a kill jar, killed a grasshopper, and made a half dozen viewer slides. Dwight seems okay, but I feel like I keep kicking this kid who is only good-hearted and well-intentioned."

"You're right," said the Leader Who is Hardly Known. "You made a mistake. Actually you made a couple of mistakes. So I'll turn your own it's-not-wrong-to-kill-nature lesson back on you. I have a lesson, too. My lesson is that I don't think it is wrong to make mistakes, but I have a rule that any time I make a mistake, I have to put that mistake to use. How can we put your lies to Dwight to good use?"

"You mean," said Mary, "what lesson did I learn in this whole mess? That's easy. Don't lie to the kids who I am teaching."

"No. You knew that before the incident occurred. What did you learn that is new?"

"Well, both lies were sort of out of desperation. I unexpectedly found myself in a desperate situation, and I tried to lie my way out of it. And to be honest, it even worked – although I feel lousy about it afterwards. I learned that I am a pretty good liar, but I don't think that's the lesson I'm supposed to get out of this."

"I don't know if every mishap has a specific lesson that you're supposed to get out of it," replied the Leader Who is Hardly Known. "Still I think that there probably is something worthwhile that you can glean from this one."

"Oh there is, now that you got me thinking about it. I did exactly what some of the kids do. I felt jammed into a corner, so out of desperation I lied. Without thinking about it, I did whatever I could to get out of my jam, even if, in retrospect, I knew it was wrong. When the kids do this, I think of them as little snots. When I do it, I feel guilty."

"So the kids might also feel guilty later..." said the Leader Who is Hardly Known.

"But," cut in Mary, "more likely they learn that lying can get them out of a jam. As a teacher, I ought to discourage this. I shouldn't let kids get away with lying."

"I'd say that you can take it a step further," said the Leader Who is Hardly Known. "You can help keep students out of positions where they might feel compelled to lie."

"You mean that I shouldn't back them into corners with unreasonable challenges," said Mary.

"That's right, although it often is hard to figure out what is reasonable and what is unreasonable. When students are pushed too hard and find themselves at their wits' end, they resort to trickery without even knowing that they are doing it.[1] Education should bring about joy, not pressure and stress. If education is stressful, then learning is diminished. If education is not fun, why would anyone seek out lifelong learning?"

## THE AFTERMATH OF CHALLENGE

*The way of the sage is the way of not attacking, not charging at his objective, not busying himself too intently about his goals.[2]*
Thomas Merton

One of the little rewards of reading for pleasure is coming across a passage that provides the key to resolving a muddled thought that long has been in the back of a person's mind. I am not talking about doing a literature review and coming across a quotation that slides nicely into a term paper. Neither am I talking about reading professional journals and finding an article with direct application to the job. These examples are too planned and too practical. I am talking about sitting in a comfortable chair, reading a novel or essay as a relaxing closure to the day, when the words on the page suddenly address something the reader has long thought about, but has never been able to articulate. Unexpectedly, an idea once vague now takes form.

One of these moments of literary serendipity happened to me with a passage from a contemporary Taoist reading called *Mentoring.*[3] At the time, I was teaching experiential education full-time and had just started taking my reading of Tao literature beyond the *Tao Te Ching* and the works of Alan Watts. Parallels between the Tao and experiential education theory already were showing themselves to me, but I had come to a conclusion that on the subject of challenge, the two simply were not in accord. Whereas challenge (i.e., coaxing students to undertake activities outside their comfort zones) was "a cornerstone of experiential education,"[4] the subject rarely came up in Tao writings – and when it did, it was in disparaging terms.[5] I sensed that there must be a link between these seemingly opposed viewpoints, but as far as my dabbling in the Tao had taken me, no common ground existed. Experiential education valued challenge and the Tao didn't. Then one night a half dozen years ago, about an hour before bed, I came across a passage that read, "In such a dynamic, spiritual relationship, we will never stop growing and expanding as we are gently pushed into waters that we once feared."[*]

Admittedly this quotation is hardly one that is going to bring most people's reading to a stop, but it certainly surprised me. For the first time in my reading about the Tao, here was a comment on challenge that read like..., well, that read... like experiential education. "Growing and expanding as we are gently pushed into waters that we once feared" immediately became my personal word puzzle. The language sounded Tao, but the sentiment, at least on first reading, did not. It was, in fact, wonderfully worded experiential education. Could it be Tao as well? There was my challenge concerning the subject of challenge.

Before presenting what I think to be the solution to this word puzzle, let me first describe the assumptions I held that prompted the conundrum in the first place. First of all, I thought that experiential education was irrevocably linked to challenge. While *learning* by experience is part of life and occurs in both challenging and non-challenging situations, experiential educators intentionally seek out the challenges in order to expedite the learning process. By placing students in unfamiliar settings and giving them problems that must be faced, these educators coerce students into thinking, choosing, and acting their way out of feelings of disequi-

---

[*] The "such" in this quote refers to the preceding paragraphs of the essay, where the authors describe a teacher-student relationship of freedom, liveliness, and energy.

libria. Experiential education follows a basic formula of 1) focus the group, 2) provide a challenging experience, and 3) debrief what occurs during the challenge. While this is an overgeneralization and an oversimplification of all that experiential education entails, no sophistication of the three steps alters the fact that challenging experiences are at the heart of the learning.[6]

Tao thinking, on the other hand, does not include challenge as a characteristic of its philosophy. If anything, challenge is to be avoided, not encouraged. According to the Tao, challenge tends to focus the participants' attention too narrowly, so they are not open to the unscripted learning opportunities that might occur. Furthermore, programs that emphasize challenge sometimes unintentionally challenge too much, and when students are too far over their heads, they do not learn at all.[7]

## The Metaphor of the Mountain

My impression was that the Tao perspective and the experiential education perspective on challenge did not have much in common. That being the case, how could a quotation that seemed to describe the experiential education approach to challenge also be a statement describing the Tao? One answer, not too surprisingly, is that the quotation can reasonably be interpreted in two different ways. One interpretation befits experiential education, the other the Tao. Here again is the quotation: "In such a dynamic, spiritual relationship, we will never stop growing and expanding as we are gently pushed into waters that we once feared."

From an experiential education perspective, the key to the quote is the gentle push. It is by gently pushing the student into unfamiliar, challenging situations that growth and expansion occur. The dynamic, spiritual relationship creates the supportive environment from which the student is pushed. The waters once feared represent the vehicle for challenge.

From the Tao perspective, however, the key is not the push, but the waters once feared. The waters have stories to tell, but they can only be heard if the student feels safe. Just as with experiential education, the dynamic, spiritual relationship provides the supportive environment, but unlike experiential education, the gentle push is just a way to get past the fear. Once the fear is gone and the student feels comfortable in the new situation, she learns what the waters have to teach. One perspective centers on the learning that occurs during the challenge. The other perspective centers on the learning that occurs in the challenge's aftermath.

For me, the difference between experiential education and the Tao on the subject of challenge is analogous to two paths leading to the summit of the same small mountain. The first route is difficult, a steep pathway that includes a technical climb up a rock face. The second route is easy in comparison to the first, a gently sloping path that gradually winds its way up the backside of the cliff. The first route attracts adventurers. These are skilled individuals with training in technical climbing. They bring climbing gear and travel considerable distances to intentionally confront the challenge of the mountain. They acknowledge the risk and take steps to minimize the most substantial dangers. They value the camaraderie of the climbing team, and they develop teamwork and self-esteem through the accomplishment of a task. The second trail appeals to wanderers. While they do not seek out the mountain, they often come upon it by chance and, without thinking much about it, take the easy way to the top. They possess no unique skills, have no special equipment, and enjoy the solitude of the winding trail. Since they do not see the mountain as a challenge to be overcome, it does not occur to them to take the difficult route.[8]

Both the adventurer and the wanderer reach the same summit taking different paths. Once on top, the adventurer basks in the afterglow of testing the outer reaches of his ability. The wanderer has no such sensation, but because she was not drawn into a challenge in the first place, is more mindful and therefore more appreciative of the mountain itself and the view that it affords. In cliché terms, the adventurer went up the mountain because it was there; the wanderer went up the mountain to see what she could see. The adventurer leaves the mountain soon after the ascent is done; the wanderer lingers and goes down only after the mountain has told its story.  The adventurer learns through the challenge of the ascent, and the wanderer learns by seeing things from a new perspective.

## A Few Concrete Examples

The lesson of the Tao perspective on challenge is a reminder that all experiential education does not have to be challenging.  In fact, if all of it is challenging, some worthwhile lessons will be lost.  While it is important to process any challenge that is faced, it is equally important to continue to experience the new situation even after it is no longer a challenge.  There is more to be learned.

The most straightforward substantiation of learning after the challenge is the teacher-student relationship itself.  Anyone who has taught knows that it is the rare teaching experience when the students actually learn more than the teacher learns.  Of course, there are overwhelming challenges faced by all novice teachers, and these challenges are the fuel of great learning, but it is once these challenges are overcome that the teacher takes his or her learning to a new level.  I know, that for me, I treasure the second, third, and fourth times that I offer a newly developed course.  The first time is bogged down by the overwhelming task of assembling a worthwhile curriculum.  By time five or six, much of the novelty has worn off, and I too often allow myself to slip into habit.  But those offerings in between!  I am very comfortable with the content, comfortable with the twists that any single class might take, and many days I walk out of class thinking, "This is education!"  I am in synch, the students are responding to my enthusiasm, and I come away with a sense of Krishnamurti's claim that the only real teachers are those who are experiencing.[9]

A very specific example of students experiencing one kind of learning through challenge and the leader experiencing another kind of learning in the challenge's aftermath is the night hike.  Night hikes may be the most consistently worthwhile activity in all of outdoor education.  For one thing, they regularly have a mystical quality to them.  Moon shadows, shooting stars, constellation myths, even the gradual onset of night vision connect people to nature in a way that daytime programming does not. One reason that night hikes have this special trait is that they are a little bit scary. Night hikes have an edge to them. Darkness, for most people, is unsettling. A learning objective of night hikes might be to achieve some kind of peacefulness, but that peacefulness is never reached without first making the unknown familiar. I have known school children who go to a camp for a week of environmental education, and the very first thing they ask as they step off the school bus is, "Do you really make us walk in the woods at night without flashlights?" For them, the night hike is a challenge. They are nervous, they put faith in their leader, and they attempt as a group something that they would never do alone as individuals. Once back in their cabins after the nighttime outing, the excitement of having faced a genuine challenge makes it just about impossible to get the kids to go to sleep. For the leader, however, the very same night hike is not an adventure at all, but a serene walk. The leader is comfortable not only because he is experienced at moving through the darkness, but also because he knows intimately the landmarks and the sounds of a place that was once a challenge. On the excursion, the kids are challenging the night, while the leader is peacefully wandering through it. The kids gain from a challenge, while the leader gains from an intimacy with nature that few people get to experience. No environmental educator worth his or her salt ever tires of nature at night.

A second specific example of learning both from challenge and post-challenge is international travel. To explain this example, the characterizations of the adventurer and the wanderer will again be useful. In terms of traveling, adventurers are the anti-tourist, intentionally avoiding international hotels and package tours, not only because such amenities insulate the visitor from the local culture, but also because adventurers want to feel the uncertainty of cutting themselves off from the security of the familiar. In fact, once a place becomes too comfortable, it is time for the adventurer to load up the backpack and move on. Ten days in Bangkok, then it is off to Hong Kong or Shanghai or Katmandu for another baptism into still another culture. Wanderers, on the other hand, are the expatriates of international travel. For them, it is only after a place starts to feel comfortable that the learning really begins.

Wanderers find apartments, have favorite restaurants, take part-time jobs, and become semi-conversant in the local language. They do not go native, but they do settle in – basically living their lives like they did back home, but in a very new setting and experiencing normalcy from a different perspective. The wanderer may experience slowly, but the places that are visited are understood well. From this example, I am tempted to say that challenge teaches breadth and after-challenge teaches depth.

## Wu Nien

Obviously experiential education is not going to abandon challenge completely and embrace a slower, gentler, more Tao-like kind of teaching. That does not mean, however, that the Tao approach to challenge has nothing to say to experiential educators. The following are two thoughts that experiential education might consider in light of the Tao perspective.

### 1. Challenge has Limits in Its Ability to Teach.

The first thing that experiential education might take from the Tao perspective on challenge is a lesson in humility, a reminder that experiential education is not the end all for education. Experiential education, so long as it uses challenge as one of its cornerstones, is only one of many ways to learn. I know that I, and this chapter may be an indication of it, tend to equate experiential education with adventure programming and outdoor education, and therefore put an emphasis on challenge. Still I must remember that challenge is not the only way to experience. While challenge teaches self-esteem, cooperation, and technical skill acquisition very well, other areas of knowledge can be taught better through other methodologies. Furthermore there are students who do not thrive in challenging environments and would learn better without feeling pushed by challenge. Conversely there are students who thrive too well in challenging environments, and feeding this mentality may not be in the students' best interests.

On two occasions, *Chuangtze* tells the allegory of the mantis. With a high opinion of its own talents, the mantis defends its territory from all intruders. It, however, has no sense of its limits, so when a chariot passes by, the mantis angrily blocks its path and, of course, is run over without even being noticed.[10] *Chuangtze* actually has a valuable message for those who go out of their way to confront risky, even dangerous, situations. That message is to slow down a bit. Because a student feels immortal does not mean that educators have to constantly put that go-for-it attitude to use. Challenge-addicted students will seldom hold back, so it falls to those responsible for the students' care to exercise restraint on their behalf. *Chuangtze* warns, "The bird flies high in the sky where it can escape the danger of stringed arrows. The field mouse burrows deep down under the sacred hill where it won't have to worry about men digging and smoking it out. Have you got less sense than these two little creatures?"[11]

## 2. Spontaneous Action Should be Valued.

One of the areas of knowledge that challenge may not address well is spontaneous action. Challenge education is a deliberate methodology.[12] It trains students to think and plan before acting. Even something as split-second as jumping off a thirty-foot pole on a ropes course is carefully considered. The hesitant student hears the facilitator's instructions, she watches other students jump off the pole, she assesses the belay system, and most notably, she musters up the courage on the ground before putting on the harnesses and confronting the challenge. The one-two-three-jump is actually the climax of a mental process that took up to thirty minutes to complete.

Not all learning, however, is so calculated. Alan Watts tells the story of a Zen master whose roof begins to leak. One of the master's students immediately grabs a sieve and places it under the spot where the water is dripping. A second student contemplates the problem, leaves and returns with a bucket. Watts claims that it might be the student with the sieve who is praised, for although the action was not appropriate, it was in the spirit of action without choosing. It is "a kind of smooth, unhesitating, flowing action in response to the challenge" that students should try to achieve. "When the moon rises, the water doesn't wait to reflect it; it reflects instantly."[13]

Watts goes on to call this freedom to act spontaneously "wu nien" and associates it with "the attitude of the unblocked mind that doesn't hesitate ever, just as the river doesn't hesitate when it flows, and just as when you clap your hands, the sound comes out without hesitation."[14] Wu nien is not seeking out challenge, but neither is it idleness or complacency. It is action, but action without consciously choosing. It is not wallowing in the familiar any more than wu-wei is doing nothing. In fact, it is moving away from the familiar and venturing into the unknown just as much as challenge does. The difference between the two is that while challenge is "going for it," wu nien is "letting go." Huang and Lynch describe it as the growth that comes about "when one is willing to let go and settle into the place of not knowing."[15]

All of us know flowing, spontaneous action when we see it. We even know it in two forms. The first is the play of young children. The actions of children sometimes make no rational sense to the orderly adult mind, but the joy and spontaneity in which they occur are the envy of every adult who still possesses a crumb of playfulness. It is, as Huizinga notes, total engagement without seriousness.[16]

The second form is the person who, when all others are either rushing around in random activity or are stunned into total inaction, calmly does what is needed. The action is immediate, but it is not rushed. It is the competent paddler among novices who navigates the rapids in the calmest, slowest, and most efficient manner. It also is the competent juggler whose fluid motions calmly bring hand after hand directly under the perfect arc of the cascading balls. In most cases, these graceful actions are the result of facing and mastering a past challenge, but instead of rushing off to stretch abilities in a new challenge, the skilled individual foregoes additional challenge to immerse himself or herself in the level that feels natural. It is, to some extent, an adult version of child's play. In the martial arts, for example, there are many degrees of black belt. At a certain point, however, promotion to the next level is not a matter of perfecting technical skills; it is turning within and mastering the Tao of the art.


## Conclusion

To some extent, the experiential education and the Tao perspectives on challenge are mirror images of each other. In experiential education, facilitators go to great effort to create a comfortable environment before taking people out of their comfort zone.[17] In Tao learning, the leader helps students work through a new situation or setting until they feel comfortable, then turns the students loose to act spontaneously. The Tao is focused on the learning that comes after the challenge has been faced or circumvented; it is the learning that comes with joyfully playing in the new situation that resides on the far side of the challenge.

Some experiential educators may not appreciate the learning that can occur within the comfort zone and, therefore, are quick to push students outside of it. They do not wonder whether it would be equally beneficial to create the comfortable setting and then forego the challenge. Wouldn't it make good sense to adequately prepare students, place them in a supportive environment, and then turn them loose to do as they please? Whereas experiential education teaches students through challenge, the Tao relies more heavily upon the setting or the environment to do the teaching. This teaching can only occur once the student feels part of that environment. In terms of the wilderness trip, it is the free day in the middle of a ten-day backpacking trip. No breaking camp, no putting in fifteen miles, no new skills training, just a day where the students are free to do whatever they want. Now comfortable in the wilderness environment, they are left to enjoy pristine nature and hopefully learn from her. Stated another way, after several days as an adventurer, students are encouraged to wander.

陰

陽

YIN/YANG

# 7

# Tao on a Tee Shirt

The Leader Who is Hardly Known was sitting at Dave's kitchen table when Dave's twelve-year-old daughter came home from school. She wore a black tee shirt with the T'ai-chi T'u (the yin/yang symbol of interlocking "tadpoles") silk-screened across the front.

"Diane," said the Leader Who is Hardly Known, "that is a wonderful tee shirt. Do you know what it means?"

"Not really. I know it's Chinese, and it means things go in circles. I just like the way it looks."

"I like the way it looks, too," said the Leader Who is Hardly Known, and he reached into the neck of his shirt and pulled out the necklace he was wearing. On the simple silver chain was a pendant of the T'ai-chi T'u.

"Oh, you have one, too," said Diane.

"Yes, a friend gave it to me a couple years ago. It was at a time when I was mad at some people who disagreed with something that I wanted to do. I wanted to teach a class about nature, and they wanted me to teach about tourism. I didn't say anything to the people who made me mad, but I complained to a friend of mine. I called the other people stupid. I said they were more worried about students getting jobs than about students learning to think. I told my friend that I wanted to quit my job and go someplace where people had their priorities straight.

"The friend then gave me this necklace. She said I was acting very strangely and that I wasn't looking at the other people's ideas.

Weren't they just as right in wanting students to have good jobs as I was in wanting them to care about nature and understand their place in the world? She gave me the necklace, so I wouldn't forget that good education is many things. The yin side could be what I wanted to teach, and the yang side could be what the other people wanted me to teach. Together the yin and yang would help the students."

The Leader Who is Hardly Known lifted the chain over his head. "Now is probably a good time to pass the necklace on. It is a present to you, and you can wear it on days that you don't wear your tee shirt."

Diane gingerly took the necklace in both hands. "Thank you," she said. "This is even better than a tee shirt. I will wear it everyday. I'm going to play now, so I'll put it in my jewelry box. Thank you." She ran out of the kitchen toward her bedroom.

Diane's father spoke up. "Now you have another friend who thinks you are acting strangely. I know you take the Tao stuff seriously, so I was a little worried when Diane charged into the house with that tee shirt on. I thought maybe you would be offended, but instead you gave her a present."

"Do you mean am I bothered that Chinese philosophy gets put on tee shirts?"

"Yeah, that people who don't know anything about the Tao use the yin and yang on tee shirts and dormitory posters."

"The yin and the yang are trendy, but I think that is a good thing. The Tao can be an esoteric philosophy locked away somewhere or it can be all over the place. Better the yin-yang symbol shows up on a tee shirt than not at all."

"You mean like Chuangtze's sacred tortoise," said Dave.

"Like what?" exclaimed the Leader Who is Hardly Known.

"Like the sacred tortoise. You're not the only one who can spout off Tao legends for every occasion. I've been reading the book you gave me."

"And what is the sacred tortoise?"

"In ancient China, turtle shells were often used in fortune telling. A diviner would move a burning stick across a treated shell, and this would cause the shell to crack in unique patterns. These patterns would then be interpreted. There, however, was a particular tortoise that was so venerated by the people that its shell was not destroyed by a burning stick. Instead its entire skeleton became a cultural relic, and it was carefully wrapped in fine silk and stored deep within the temple where no one could damage it or, for that matter, even see it. Still, had anyone bothered to ask the tortoise for its opinion, it surely would have chosen to be neither a relic nor a divining oracle, but would have preferred remaining an unremarkable living tortoise dragging its tail through the mud."[1]

"So," said the Leader Who is Hardly Known, "better on a tee shirt on a kid who rolls around in the mud than tucked away where no one sees it."

"Better," said the friend, "to be a little tattered around the edges and known to all than to be perfect, but made available to no one."

 THE YIN AND THE YANG

> At midday, the sun begins to set; once the moon is full, it begins to wane. This cycle of yin and yang, filling and emptying, waxing and waning, is an established, unchanging pattern.
>
> Lui I-ming

Of all Tao concepts, the yin-yang is the most familiar to Westerners. It, along with its symbolic representation (called the T'ai-chi T'u), has become part of popular culture. The yin and the yang serve as a useful shorthand to describe opposites that complement each other (e.g., she is the yin to his yang). More importantly, the yin and the yang have gained recognition in the West because they offer an alternative to the values and attitudes that have dominated Western thinking for the past few centuries.

The dominant Western perspective is dualistic. It tends to put things in either/or categories. Something is good or it is bad, not both good and bad. Something is masculine or it is feminine, not both masculine and feminine. The dominant Western philosophy also is hierarchical. Humans are over nature. Masculine is over feminine. Developed nations are over developing nations. This dominant dualistic and hierarchical system is male-oriented and rational. It is aggressive. It has great faith in science. It believes that time and events progress linearly, with a beginning, a middle, and an end, as opposed to moving cyclically. The dominant philosophy consistently gives very little credence to feminine perspectives, to intuition and inspiration, to passiveness, to spirituality, and to cyclical events.

From a Taoist perspective, this kind of Western thinking is flawed, not because it is male, rational, scientific, and aggressive, but because it is only male, rational, scientific, and aggressive. It has been all yang and no yin. The yin-yang concept of complementary opposites offers an alternative theory to those who sense that unquestioning faith in a single way of thinking limits options and has been the source of many of the inequities in Western society.[3]

UNITY AND BALANCE

There are two characteristics of the yin-yang principle that highlight its differences from Western dualism. The first is what Alan Watts called the "duality expressing an implicit unity."[4] According to Tao thinking, opposites are not separate, disconnected, either/or elements, but are two parts of a single entity. Maleness cannot be separated from femaleness. Rational thinking cannot be separated from intuitive thinking. Opposites are extremes on a single continuum, and one half of a continuum cannot exist without the other half.

When extreme opposites are no longer looked at as separate and distinct, but as distant points on a single continuum, then most things in life do not appear as those distant points, but as something in between. They are not either/or, good or bad, but a blend of their complementary opposites. For example, masculine men reveal a nurturing side when holding their young children. Developed landscapes contain elements of nature in their design. Traditional classrooms include some experiential learning.

A second important characteristic that helps to distinguish the yin-yang principle from its Western counterpart is the concept of dynamic balance. This means that entities in balance are in constant motion, yet remain in equilibrium. From a yin-yang perspective, balance does not mean finding the perfect spot on a continuum and holding to that spot come hell or high water. It also does not mean choosing one extreme over the other and constantly pushing in only one direction. Balance is recognizing that an ebb and flow is natural and inevitable, and balance is maintained by adjusting to the movement and the change. It is the failure to adjust that leads to problems.

> ...yang energy without restraint turns into aggressiveness, like fire rising. Yin energy is flexible; flexibility without support becomes too weak, like water descending. When firmness and flexibility do not balance each other, solitary yin cannot give life, isolated yang cannot foster growth – so living energy ceases.[5]

In the West, an easing of the dualistic and hierarchical grip is occurring, even if the change is gradual. The civil rights movement, the environmental movement, the feminist movement, and the increased acceptance of spirituality by Western civil institutions are indications of a yin influence. Overall an unquestioned faith in a yang perspective is waning, and the pendulum is starting to swing back toward the philosophical/intuitive side of the spectrum. For example, scientific accomplishments such as genetic engineering reveal that science without discussion of moral implications is corrupt. This is not to say that faith in science is not still dominant, but there is a general recognition that a faith in science is not enough to solve the problems that science and technology have helped to create. *Time* Magazine named Albert Einstein the Person of the Century because *Time*'s editors believed that the Twentieth Century, more than anything else, would be remembered as the age of science and technological development. It is just as likely that the Twentieth Century will be remembered as the moment in history when faith in science and technology was taken to its farthest extremes.

A small, yet concrete, example of the shifting pendulum is the 2000 Census in the United States. For the first time ever, people of mixed ancestry were allowed to check more than one box in the race category. Prior to 2000, individuals of more than one race had only two options – check one of their races (white, black, Native American, Asian, Hispanic, or Pacific Islander) or check "other." With the new census, people no longer have to identify themselves as either/or. The fuzziness of the line that has always existed is finally being acknowledged.

## YIN-YANG AND EXPERIENTIAL EDUCATION

The introduction of this book mentioned that experiential education has much in common with the Tao. Nowhere is this more evident than with the yin-yang principle. In fact, if there is a single piece of writing that effectively links one aspect of Tao thinking to its counterpart in experiential education, it is Hua-ching Ni's definition of the yin and the yang. In *Entering the Tao*, he wrote:

> *Yang signifies something causing change. Perceptible change is the criterion that lets us infer that "action" has taken place. The yin quality describes something tending to transform a momentary phenomenon into a persistent one; it lets fleeting qualities endure... Yang implies creation and generation, whereas yin nourishes and supports growth.*[6]

Ni could have been describing the connection between the action phase and the reflective phase of experiential education programming. The yang, or the action, causes change and alerts students that change is occurring. The yin, or the reflection, organizes the action so that its lessons stay with the students even after the action is over. If a program was only action after action after action, participants would move forward and progress, but that progress might not have direction. At the very least, many participants would not realize the implications of what was occurring. Conversely, if a program was entirely reflection, it would take on an ivory tower mentality; i.e., great ideas would be generated, but then not tested in real world situations. Action followed by reflection followed by action... may be slower than pure action and less insightful than pure reflection, but it is the way to bring about both change and an understanding of that change. As stated in the anonymously written One Hundred Proverbs, "Keep your mind busy to accomplish things; keep your mind open to understand things."[7]

Every seasoned experiential educator knows well that the action component of an experience usually is much easier to facilitate than the reflection or processing phase. I have always assumed that the reason for this difference is that facilitating the action can become relatively routine, whereas the processing is unique each time it is done. Roman Catholic monk and Tao scholar, Thomas Merton, suggested that another reason for action coming easy and processing hard is that action comes naturally to people and reflection does not. Merton may have overstated it when he described reflection (the act of resting) as "the hardest and most courageous act (a person) can perform," but made a valid point in noting that most people most of the time move from experience to experience without pondering the implications.

For a good share of the time, not bothering to reflect is appropriate. Many actions of daily life are fairly mundane and do not have a great deal to teach. Even Merton observed that, "Life is not a matter of getting something out of everything."[8] Failure to reflect, however, can become habit, and then even quality experiences do not get the reflection they deserve. When this happens, quality is not distinguished from the dull and routine, and potential lessons are lost. Merton made this exact point in Tao-like language when he wrote, "As long as we are not in our own possession, all our activity is futile. If we let all our wine run out the barrel and down the street, how will our thirst be quenched?"[9]

If it is correct that a lack of reflection is keeping people from learning the lessons of life, then the use of processing within experiential education takes on new significance. It no longer is just a technique for revealing to students the lessons of a specific facilitated action; it is an example of the importance of reflection. Educators teach skills in the hopes that use of those skills continues after the formal schooling is over. In experiential education, for example, backpacking skills are taught so that students will continue to backpack on their own, and team-building skills are taught so that a group continues to work together even after the facilitator is no longer around to facilitate cooperation. If reflection is as important in daily life as outdoor skills and team-building, then processing is no longer just a tool to be used by the facilitator; it is a trainable skill that should be passed on to students so that they continue to reflect after the instruction is over.

In other words, an underappreciated responsibility of quality experiential education is to encourage students to take reflection seriously and to teach them to reflect well. This task has several components to it. First of all, it requires that experiential educators continually provide action that is good enough and complex enough to merit reflection. Few things are more torturous for both facilitator and student than processing the mundane. It is processing for the sake of processing even when the action has little to teach. Second, a good processing session is not only a reflection of the immediate action, but also a lesson in processing. Through the processing session, students do learn something about the action just completed, but equally important, they witness an example of quality reflection. Good processing teaches the art of reflecting, so students are more apt to process when not under the guidance of a teacher. Third, facilitators need to teach students that reflection is worth the effort. Processing sessions must be interesting in and of themselves. They must, as much as possible, reveal aspects of the completed action that otherwise would not be realized. In some, but not all instances, processing should be fun. This means using various processing methods instead of relying solely on straight question and answer. Fourth and finally, quality processing should help students determine the experiences that are deserving of reflection and those that are not. This is difficult, and while I have no specific suggestions as to how to accomplish it, I suspect that part of it is processing only when there is something worthwhile to process.

## The Yin of Education

A reasonable question to ask about teaching reflection is "Why does the responsibility fall to experiential education? If this is so important, shouldn't it be the job of all education?" The answer to the question is, "Yes, something as important as reflection should be taught in all educational methodologies. To some extent, it is. But the task of teaching reflection will fall most heavily on experiential education. It all goes back to the yin and the yang. Reflection is the yin of the action/reflection continuum, and experiential education is the yin of education. What better way to set an example of the yin than the yin itself?"

Is experiential education really the yin of education? At first thought, this seems to contradict the yin/yang balance within experiential education's one-two punch of processing and action. Actually both statements are true. In other words, while experiential education has components of both the yin and the yang, it is the yin of education. In its own microcosm, experiential education is a balance of yin and yang. The action is yang-like, the processing yin. Experiential education, however, does not exist in a vacuum. Besides something that can be looked at as a self-contained entity, experiential education also is part of a larger body that encompasses all educational methodologies. Within that bigger world, especially when compared to traditional education, experiential education is yin.

Experiential education is yin for the very fact that it values reflection so highly. Even though much of experiential education is action and therefore yang, it is during moments of reflection that most of the learning occurs. If all of life's experiences were experiments, then they would produce objective, quantifiable results, and reflection would rarely be required. Such reflection would be arguing hard facts. Our world, however, is not a laboratory, our experiences cannot be replicated with any precision, and we cannot predict how each of life's happenings is going to turn out. Therefore, subjective reflection is the path for interpreting our experiences, and such things as gut feelings, inspiration, and intuitive intelligence all contribute to the reflective process.[10]

Table 1 describes experiential education and traditional education from a yin-yang perspective. Keep in mind that the table is listing extremes, two ends of a continuum. Most education is not wholly experiential, nor wholly traditional, so any specific education programming is, as Hua-ching Ni noted, "composed of unequal proportions of yin and yang."[11]

## TABLE 1. THE YIN AND YANG OF EDUCATION

| EXPERIENTIAL EDUCATION (YIN) | TRADITIONAL EDUCATION (YANG) |
|---|---|
| Concerned Primarily in the Process | Concerned Primarily in the End Result |
| Direct Experience in Reality | Abstractions & Symbols of Reality |
| Intuitive Knowledge | Rational Knowledge |
| Feeling | Intellectualizing |
| Cycles of Action/Reflection | Movement from Grade to Grade |
| Synthesis | Analysis |
| Cooperation & Teamwork | Individual Effort & Accomplishment |
| Flexibility | Schedules and Standards |
| Uniqueness of Each Group/Individual | Conformation to Societal Standards |
| Reflection | Standardized Testing |

## CONCLUSION

One reason that experiential education theory has so much in common with Tao thinking is that both are yin-like. As experiential education is the yin of education, Tao is the yin of Chinese philosophy (with Confucianism its yang complement). Table 1 applies as well to Tao/Confucianism as it does to experiential education/traditional education.[12] Still Tao thinking is quick to point out that learning from only a yin perspective leads to an incomplete education. As Liu I-ming put it, "If learners can blend yin and yang without partiality or bias, ending up in correct balance, then the heart of heaven and earth will reappear."[13]

This does not mean, however, that any one educator needs to offer a full spectrum, a mix of yin and yang, within his or her instruction. No class or program, even an exceptional one, can do everything well. Experiential educators, for example, fulfill their educational responsibility by exposing students to the yin of teaching, but always with an awareness that their methodologies are only one piece of the learning puzzle. In fact, the best experiential educators are those who study, understand, and appreciate many approaches to education (including traditional education), for they are the ones who best see where experiential education fits into the mix.

In "Autumn Floods," *Chuangtze* told the story of the Spirit of the River, who was so in awe of Confucian thought that he would not listen to ideas that differed from the great teacher's wisdom. Then the Spirit of the River journeyed to the sea, and it realized that all rivers, no matter how great, were small compared to the water where all rivers flowed. When the Spirit of the Ocean saw what the Spirit of the River had learned, it said, "A frog in a well can't have much to say about the sea. It's bound by its own empty space. A summer bug won't have much to say about ice. It's trapped in its tiny time. A cloistered scholar can't have much to say about the Tao, being all wrapped up in his doctrine and dogma. Now that you have seen the great sea (the big picture), you know your own insignificance and can begin to speak of great principles." The Spirit of the Ocean then went on to say that every tool does something well, and to rely on only one is inconsistent with the Tao. In fact, to choose one style of teaching and reject another "is like saying that heaven's your teacher, but not earth; or yin, but not yang. There is no possibility of such thinking getting anyone into the light, but they keep talking that way nonetheless."[14]

LEADERSHIP

# 8

# The Evacuation

The Leader Who is Hardly Known watched one hundred-eighty kids eating breakfast in the environmental center's dining hall. A storm during the night had knocked out the electricity, but the kids hardly noticed the difference. Rain beat on the building's roof, and the natural lighting through the windows was subdued because of heavy cloud cover. The Leader Who is Hardly Known knew that he needed to call a quick meeting of the staff to discuss how the inclement weather and the lack of electrical power was going to affect the day's activities.

Just then Chris, the assistant director, walked up alongside him. She wore a worried look on her face and said, "I just heard the weather report, and the storm is going to get worse. There is no way that we can go to the tide pools today, but I'm even thinking that we should consider sending all of the kids home. If we have another mudslide across the camp road, it would be four or five days before we could get the kids out, even longer before we'd get electricity back."

It was Wednesday, and the session was scheduled to run until Friday morning. Chris went on, "Heavy rains will continue for forty-eight hours, winds will pick up with gusts up to seventy miles an hour. Even if the kids stay, it would be dangerous to wander any distance from the buildings."

"Okay," said the Leader Who is Hardly Known. "Send Derek and Rachel in to finish supervising breakfast. Have the rest of the staff meet in the kitchen office in ten minutes. I'll have Derek and Rachel keep the kids and the counselors in the dining hall until we figure out what to do."

After a short discussion with the staff, the Leader Who is Hardly Known decided to send the kids home. The decision did not have full support. The entire season was booked, so once the kids left camp they probably would not get another chance to come back. Still once the decision was made, everyone just wanted to know what they needed to do to facilitate the evacuation.

"Chris," said the Leader Who is Hardly Known, "How should we do this?"

"First," said Chris, "we need to explain to the kids what we are doing and why we are doing it. Tell them the truth without scaring them. Then we need to send them all back to their cabins to pack. While they are packing, some of us can take down the tables in the dining hall, so the kids can bring their gear indoors and put it in piles according to their schools. Someone needs to call each of the schools to tell them that the kids are coming home. People in the school offices can get in touch with the kids' parents. I need to call the school bus companies that brought the kids and have them send buses to pick the kids up. The office phone is out, but we can use my cell phone. I think, however, that we should use our own bus to take the kids from Stockton home. They live too far away. It'd take four hours for a bus from Stockton to get here. That's too long. The round trip will take all day, so that will cut into the bus company's afternoon school runs. They might not even have a driver available. Most of us need to entertain the kids until the buses come, but we need to do it by school rather than cabin group. That way we can quickly load up kids when a bus from a particular school shows. We need to keep tabs on the weather, but I think that we will be okay if we act this morning."

"Jeeze, Chris," said George, one of the other staff, "have you been planning this evacuation for a month?" The staff laughed, and Chris blushed.

"Well, no..." Chris stammered, "but it does seem like a good way to go."

"It seems like a perfect way to go," said the Leader Who is Hardly Known. "I will drive the bus to Stockton. Margaret, would you

ride on the bus with me and the kids?  Depending on road conditions, we might not get back until late – and if there is a mudslide,
we might not get back at all."  After Margaret nodded her head,
the Leader went on, "That's it.  I'll go out and talk to the kids.  The
rest of you stay here, so Chris can give you your duties.  I don't like
doing this, but I think that we err on the side of caution."

The drive to Stockton took much longer than expected.  First of all,
the winds were so strong for a while that the Leader pulled the bus
over and waited.  Then because of that delay, several toilet stops
became necessary.  After the kids were unloaded at their school,
Margaret and the Leader Who is Hardly Known called Chris on her
mobile phone to learn that all the kids from the other schools were
home safely.  Then they stopped at a restaurant to eat and to rest
up before starting the drive home.

After they had ordered their food, Margaret said, "I think that it is
kind of weird that you drove the bus and left Chris in charge at
camp.  I know that the two of you are the only ones with bus driver
licenses, but why didn't you stay and have Chris drive?"

"Why do you think I should have stayed in camp?"

"Because you're the boss, I guess," said Margaret.

"I am the boss," said the Leader Who is Hardly Known, "so I del-
egated evacuation responsibilities to the person who I thought
would do the best job.  Someone who I thought would do a better
job than me.  That was Chris."

"I guess," said Margaret.  "She was in her element, wasn't she?
Usually I think Chris is too anal.  No, that's not fair – usually I
think that she is too regimented, but she is wonderful when we
need orderliness.  While I am still trying to understand the problem, she already has a plan all figured out."

"That's right.  I would never have thought of using our own bus to
take home the kids who lived the farthest away, but as soon as she
said it, everyone knew that was the right thing to do.  Chris won't
relax until she has personally checked that every task has been

completed to her satisfaction. I am sure that she made every phone call, double checked that every kid got out of camp, and made sure that every bus made it safely back to its school. She probably even lectured the rest of the staff about where they should and shouldn't go once the kids left camp."

"Yeah, but I bet she didn't tell them a bedtime story. That's your job."

"Yes, it is. My strengths lie in showing the staff and the kids that they are important and in showing them that the natural environment is important. I paint with a broad brush and sometimes miss the details. Chris pays the bills, maintains service records on the bus, and fills in as nurse when Anita is offsite. She probably cares more about the center than any of us, but because she is not as bubbly and huggy as the rest of the staff, she is not always appreciated as much as she should be. Some talented individuals are complete leaders. I am not, but that doesn't matter at all if we have and use the characteristics of a complete leader within the talents of all of our staff."

## BOTH A LEADER AND A MANAGER

*When ruler and minister differ in their ways, there is order; when they make their ways identical, there is disorder.*[1]

Huainanzi

In *The Importance of Living*, Lin Yutang cautions the reader not to take anything, even the Tao, to extremes. To do so, paradoxically, is not Tao-like. Extreme Taoism leads to perfect peace, but it does not lead to the Tao because it separates a person from everyday life. "It is," according to Lin, "poor philosophy that teaches us to escape from human society altogether."[2]

This chapter is the experiential education equivalent of Lin's warning in that it suggests not taking the concept of the leader-who-is-hardly-known to extremes. It is, I suppose, the disclaimer of the book and should come with a proviso that reads "The author and publisher of this book assume no responsibility for experiential educators who abandon all order and practicality so as to be one with the Tao." The Tao is an excellent perspective for experiential educators to learn from, but it is not a complete guide. It is, after all, a philosophy, and "philosophy bakes no bread."[3] On the topic of leadership, for example, Tao writings exhibit the same shortcoming as many leadership textbooks; that is they make a distinction between leadership and management, claim both are important, and then speak only to leadership. The leadership textbooks leave it to the management texts to discuss administrative detail. Tao writings leave it, I guess, to Confucius.

## A Mention of Management within the Tao

The way that Tao writings deal with the practicalities of leadership is to delegate them to a subordinate administrative level and then leave it at that. For example, the *Chuangtze* states, "The essentials lie with the ruler; the details lie with the subjects."[4] This, however, is a bothersome passage. It is hierarchical and a bit arrogant. It seems very un-Tao to call some responsibilities essential and others something less. Because this quote comes from the Outer Chapters of the *Chuangtze*, which means Chuangtze himself did not write it, I was tempted to ignore it as a mistake or an anomaly. My inclination to ignore the quote, which was a dubious approach in the first place, fell apart when I found the same sentiment showing up in other Tao works. The *Huainanzi*, for example, not only acknowledges the need for a managerial level under the Tao leader, but also points out that the personality and methods of the manager must differ from those of the person at the top. The *Huainanzi* states:

> The way of the ruler is round, revolving endlessly, with a nurturing spiritual influence, open and selfless, harmonious, always in the background and never in the forefront. The way of the minister is square, deliberating on what is right and applying appropriate measures, initiating suggestions for action, keeping to the job with distinct clarity, thus achieving success.... When they each manage to do what is appropriate for them and handle their own responsibilities, then superior and subordinate have the means to work together.[5]

Even one interpretation of the *Tao Te Ching*'s Chapter 17 alludes to the need for a manager to carry out logistics in behalf of the top-most leader. Chapter 17 is, of all things, the section of the *Tao Te Ching* from which the phrase "The Leader Who is Hardly Known" comes. Most English translations interpret Chapter 17 to mean that a person in authority might choose to be one of four kinds of leader, the best being a leader who is hardly noticed by his or her followers. For example, the Henry Wei translation reads:

> The best rulers are not known to the people;
> Then come those who are loved and praised;
> Then those who are held in awe;
> And lastly those who are despised.[6]

Translator R. B. Blakney, however, sees the chapter differently. Acknowledging that Tao leadership needs both the visionary and the manager, Blakney interprets the chapter not as a choice of four styles of leadership for the topmost leader, but as four tiers of leadership within a single organization, each level being perceived differently by those being served. Blakney's translation reads:

> As for him who is highest,
> The people just know he is there.
> His deputy's cherished and praised;
> Of the third, they are frightened;
> The fourth, they despise and revile.[7]

In his commentary on the chapter, Blakney wrote, "In the hierarchy of government, the king is only a name to the people; his deputy is loved and praised because the people want to have faith in some-one high in government; the third in command is more familiar but still out of reach and so he is feared; the man in the fourth grade down from majesty is on the firing line and will be the target for all who are vexed."[8] While Blakney's translation is out of the ordinary and does not coincide with a literal word-by-word transla-tion of the Chinese, the result is not unreasonable.* It is consis-tent with a notion that, while a ruler can remain a free-flowing and Tao-like figure, someone needs to address the particulars of run-ning a government or organization.

## The Yang of Experiential Education?

So where does this suggestion of a leadership hierarchy leave experiential education? Tao writings say little about managerial responsibilities, but duties such as establishing guidelines, keeping track of records and statistics, putting vision into action, and doing a good job with the important, but sometimes tedious, things that allow an organization to function, are hardly responsibilities that experiential education can ignore. Certainly a go-with-the-flow everything-will-work-out attitude can be taken too far. Anyone who has attended a workshop or gone on a backpacking trip that has no itinerary knows this to be true. Experiential education and Tao leadership work only if there is something that holds things together and addresses the details. Obviously the trick is to have the structure of an orderly program without sacrificing too much spontaneity.

One way to balance the free flow of the Tao with structure and orderliness is to have two personalities at the top of an organization. Those two personalities might be one exceptional person who can move back and forth from idealistic role model to logistician, but more likely it is two different people working together to become the complete leader/administrator. The *Chuangtze* and *Huainanzi* clearly state that the topmost leader should be the Tao-like visionary and the second in command the person carrying out the vision. At the risk of contradicting these Tao classics, I am not sure that experiential education needs to be so inflexible in its leadership configuration. I can't speak for ruling a nation, but in experiential education, it does not seem to matter who is the big picture person and who is the administrator, so long as both jobs get done. In fact, the assistant director frequently is promoted to director. Is it realistic to expect a person who has been asked to be the organization's bean counter for years to suddenly transform into a role model visionary?

I suspect that a good situation in experiential education is when the director and assistant director tend to ignore the distinction in their

---

* I used eight English interpretations and a word-by-word translation of the *Tao Te Ching* in writing this book. Only the Blakney translation interpreted Chapter 17 in this way.

two titles.  Everyone else, even the rest of the staff, might see one person in charge and a second person in a secondary role, but the two individuals see the roles as co-facilitators.  For example, I once participated in a rafting trip on the San Juan River of Utah where the designated leader of the trip was definitely the manager of the excursion.  She supervised the packing of the rafts, she determined the itinerary, she directed the staff, and she provided instruction to the participants.  It was the assistant leader who was hardly known, and while he did not exert any more authority on the participants than a junior-level staff member, he served as the philosophical and emotional advisor for the trip.  He clearly was aware of everything that was occurring.  He identified and befriended the misfit participants on the trip, he immediately moved to the side of the leader whenever an unexpected situation occurred, and he possessed, but never flaunted, the best technical skills of anyone on the river.  This assistant leader possessed a calmness that I've rarely seen in a person anywhere, no less in a person who was leading an excursion into a desert wilderness.  Even though I expressly went on the trip to observe the trip leaders as a way to improve my own leadership skills, I revealed my own novice status as a leader by being well into the trip before realizing that the assistant leader was key to the success of the whole expedition.

Structure and orderliness come not only from detail-oriented individuals, but also from the configuration of the organization itself.  The *Sun Tzu*, a 3rd Century Chinese text of military strategy, points out that the positive traits of leaders have value only if there is an organization in place that puts those traits to use.  "The ruler is powerful because he is at the head of a complex set of relationships.  By contrast, personal strength, morality and ability are qualities that belong only to the individual.  They are ineffective unless conjoined with the larger patterns of influence."[9]

The *Sun Tzu* description, while not very specific, does suggest a typical experiential education program.  The instructors frequently are individuals of moral character and unique skills, and even though they often are disordered and a bit rough around the edges, the structure of the program sees that these unorthodox individuals have a positive impact on the students that they serve.  The structure of the program actually gives these teachers a freedom that they may not otherwise have. They can be spontaneous, idealistic, even a bit naîve in their romanticism, but still remain effective because the program is credible. I understand that good people make good programs, but it also works in reverse, i.e., established, respected programs allow good people the freedom to try new things without fear of harming the organization.

For example, back in my early days as an environmental educator in northern California, my fellow naturalists and I were an odd mix of environmentalists living deep in the redwood forests of the Santa Cruz Mountains. We were seen as so out-of-the-mainstream by our students that we could stun them just by showing up in a local movie theatre or shopping mall. The kids saw us as Grizzly Adams-type characters who belonged in the woods and not the local Cineplex. The environmental education program that we worked for, however, was part of the public school system. There were school officials miles away from our facility who raised funds, attended board meetings, and constantly explained the value of non-traditional education to parents, school boards, and other educational administrators. While the naturalists sometimes resented the restrictions that our school affiliation put on the program, we realized that the continued existence of the environmental education center depended on that affiliation. We could get away with being experientially-oriented tree huggers because our institutional links to the County Department of Education made us credible.

## CONCLUSION

For all of its strengths, Tao thinking does tend to ignore the role of management in quality leadership. I am sure that the more matter-of-fact readers of this book are way ahead of me on this observation. Since the first couple of chapters they have been thinking, "All of this theory is interesting, but where's the practicality of it? Being humble, being open, being tolerant are good, but these generalities are telling me nothing about day-to-day operations. I've got program objectives and specific tasks to accomplish. Who's making the staff schedule and who's keeping track of staff certifications and who's making sure that we don't lose any kids in the woods while I am off getting in touch with my yin side?"

Experiential educators carry a lot of responsibility. They often facilitate activities that, if not done correctly, are dangerous. They often work with adjudicated youth and others who have not fared well in more traditional education settings and need close supervision. They occasionally find themselves in situations where one person needs to take total charge, and all others need to follow orders without question. They almost always are involved in activities where their skill level exceeds the others in the group, and the less skilled naturally turn to them for guidance.

With all of this responsibility and with all of this need to take charge, experiential educators must always consider how far they can take the concept of a leader who is hardly known. The only recommendation that I can make concerning this balancing act is to use common sense. It is, I think, right to be a leader who is hardly known, but it is not always *reasonable* to be one. If this statement seems contradictory, consider whether a country can be right, but not reasonable, to start a war, or whether a person can be right, but not reasonable, to hold steadfastly to an extreme political view. Lin Yutang once wrote that the greatest thing Chinese philosophy offers is "the spirit of reasonableness." Something is not judged right or wrong, logical or illogical. It is simply seen as reasonable or unreasonable. Westerners, Lin claimed, are too concerned with being right. They take a stand, then devise an argument defending that stand, usually at the expense of hearing the strengths of a different perspective and often in opposition to doing what is reasonable.[10] It is good to be Tao-like, but above all, an effective leader must be reasonable.

APPROPRIATE TIMING

# 9

# Birdwatching at Fifty

As a trip for seeing birds, the Leader Who is Hardly Known knew it had been a successful walk in the marsh. He and a group of a fourteen young adults had identified over two dozen species of birds, among them great blue herons, common egrets, and wood ducks. As a nature appreciation experience, however, the trip had failed. The processing session after the walk confirmed this.

"You seemed to get into birdwatching," Kelly, one of the participants, said to the Leader Who is Hardly Known, "but to be honest, I was bored."

Paul, the only student who did seem interested in the birds, spoke up. "I disagree. I thought it was great! I had seen most of those birds before, but except for the mallards and the red-winged blackbirds, I didn't know what they were called. More importantly, I saw more stuff today than I ever had before. That pied-billed grebe, for example. It was in plain sight, but I would have paid it no attention had I not been birdwatching. I felt like I finally opened my eyes, and there was twice as much to see as before. Tonight I am going to buy a pair of binoculars and a bird book."

"Well, for me, it was a letdown," said Kelly. "Last week we went caving. The week before that we canoed. The week before that we rock climbed. Our trips are the highlight of my week, so maybe I was expecting too much. Birdwatching has no adventure to it. I can see how some people get into it, but it's something I won't do until I'm fifty."

Further discussion showed that Kelly's viewpoint represented the group. For all students other than Paul, birdwatching lacked excitement. It was something that they might do later in life, but not now.

"Your comments are interesting," said the Leader Who is Hardly Known. "They remind me of two other birding trips that I have done. The first was not supposed to be a birding trip, but turned out to be. It was a training session for staff at an environmental education center. I had taken the new employees, a group of about this size and about this age, to a salt marsh ten miles from the center. The purpose of the trip was to show the new staff the trails in the marsh, the ecological concepts usually covered there, and a few easy activities they might do with a group of children. The excursion, however, quickly elevated or degenerated, depending on your perspective, into a birding trip. The salt marsh was alive with birds. Wading birds, swimming birds, marsh wrens, gulls, marsh hawks — for a person interested in birding, the place was paradise. As it turned out, about half of the new staff members were birders, and half didn't know a duck from a swan and didn't care. For an hour, six people were having a day to remember. Another six were bored to tears. These were not just people off the street, but people training to be professional naturalists. Even among this group, birding was an acquired taste.

"The second birding trip that I recall was a planned outing. A friend of mine had received binoculars for a birthday present, and she asked if I would introduce her to birdwatching. As this was her first time out, I thought a large city park would be fine as a start. I was living in San Francisco at the time, so we went to Golden Gate Park. For an urban setting, Golden Gate Park is a good place to bird.

About an hour into our walk, my friend was leafing through her guide to identify a bird. I was looking over her shoulder and was pleased to see that she had turned to the right page on her own.

"Oh, my God! Oh, my God! Is that the bird?" she asked, as she pointed to a sketch of a large brown finch that is very common to the Bay Area.

"Sure," I said. "Why is that so exciting?"

"My God," she said for the third time. "Two or three months ago, my husband and I were babysitting a friend's three-year-old daughter for the day. We took her to the zoo. While we were eating lunch at a picnic table, a small bird was flitting around on the ground around us. Barbara, the little girl, looked at the bird and cried out "Too-eee, too-eee!" I corrected her and said, "No Barbie, that's a birdy." She then pointed at the bird and said, "Too-eee." She was pointing at the same bird as this one. It's a towhee. A brown towhee. My God, that little kid was a human bird identification guide, and I was telling her to call it a birdy."

"Consider the salt marsh and the Golden Gate Park examples," continued the Leader Who is Hardly Known. "In one instance, professional naturalists-in-training were not interested in birding. In another, a three-year old child already could name the birds in her neighborhood. So the question is, when are people ready to learn a particular activity? While I do not know the answer to that question, age obviously is not the only indicator.

"Today all of you taught me a valuable lesson. I do not regret that we went birdwatching. Paul may have found a new lifelong hobby. The rest of you gave up only three hours, and this birding trip may coax you into birdwatching ten, twenty, thirty years from now. Still I don't think that I will include birdwatching in the course next semester. The purpose of today's class was to encourage you to notice nature at a greater intensity than you had previously – and that didn't happen. Except for Paul, you were bored. You walked along with me, but mostly you were talking about movies and restaurants and plans for tonight. I believe that, with perhaps few exceptions, educators should teach a topic only when the students are ready to learn it. For now, I'll grab your attention with carabineers and canoes, have binoculars handy while we are on our adventures, and trust that the rest will come with time."

# 適
# 師 TEACH WHEN THE TIME IS RIGHT

*When one's thoughts and experience have not reached a certain point for reading a masterpiece, the masterpiece will leave only a bad flavor on his palate.*[1]

Lin Yutang

Many adults wish that, as children, they had learned a particular skill that would be of use to them now. These people can, without a moment' s hesitation, fill in the blank to the sentence, "I wish that I had learned to _____ when I was a kid." The blank might be filled with play the piano or swim or cook well by having paid more attention to activities in the kitchen.

In my own case, I wish that I had learned to speak and read Chinese when I was young. My work and my personal interests increasingly draw me to Taiwan, to the People's Republic of China, and to the Chinese community in the United States, so I have been struggling for years to take my language skills to something beyond survival Mandarin Chinese. However, as much as I wish that I had learned Chinese at an earlier age, I also realize that it never would have happened growing up in Wisconsin during the 1950's and 60's. As a kid, my sense of globalization was watching the Vietnam War on television and going on fishing trips to Canada. Who in the relatively provincial city of Green Bay, Wisconsin, whether my parents or anyone else, would have stopped me from playing in the woods to come indoors and work on my Chinese lessons? To the credit of all the adults with an impact on my childhood, they knew that my time in the woods was time well spent.

Each learning opportunity comes in its own time. This does not mean that the appropriate mentor or lesson or book magically materializes just at the time that a person needs it, but that the alert mind seeks out that mentor, lesson, or book when the time is right. The reason that I didn't study Chinese earlier in life is because now is the time that I want to understand Chinese. For me, learning Chinese finally has purpose, so I'm finally willing to put in the hours and hours it takes to get a handle on the language. In fact, had I been cooped up indoors studying Chinese as a child, it is possible that the course of events that brought me to needing Chinese would never have occurred. It was because I was free to run around in the woods near my home when I was in grade school that I developed a love of nature at an early age. That love of nature led to my university studies in outdoor recreation. Because of that training, I was invited to Taiwan to teach outdoor recreation and environmental education. And only because of the opportunities afforded me through my two years in Taiwan do I feel that I need to improve my comprehension of the Chinese language. Therefore, if I had studied Chinese as a child or adolescent, my Chinese lessons might have gone the way of my high school French courses – forgotten now because I took the courses only on a guidance counselor's recommendation. Each thing comes in its own time.

The concept that we learn best when the time is right is consistent with Tao thinking. We learn what we need to learn when we need to learn it. According to the Tao, wisdom does not come by following a rigid predetermined plan and timeline. It is reached by emulating the rivers and seas, for they "come to be known for their merits by a natural process of development."[2] From the viewpoint of a teacher, this means that it is not a valuable use of time to jam a lesson down a student's throat before he or she is ready to learn it. In the previous paragraph, I said that the alert student might seek out a mentor when the time is right. From the mentor's perspective, responsibility to that student is to be available when the student is seeking guidance and/or to help that student get to the point where he or she realizes what help is needed. As Krishnamurti described it, "We [as teachers] no longer want to transform the individual into something else; our only concern is to help him understand himself."[3]

## AN EXPERIENTIAL EDUCATION LEAP OF FAITH

None of us can predict what we will want to know twenty years in the future, but that does not mean that educators wait for twenty years to start teaching. Traditional education certainly does not wait. It makes calculated guesses at what the majority of us will need in the future – language skills, mathematics, history, ethics and civic responsibility, computer skills – and trusts that these general skills will serve as a foundation regardless of the path each of us takes and will serve us when we finally figure out the specifics of what we need to live our lives.

Of course, there are mistakes in this calculated fortune telling. For example, college students of my generation used huge stacks of data entry cards in their computer science courses and graduated with less computer literacy than many of today's kindergartners. Still, much of what we learn in traditional school proves to have some practical value. No matter what any of us do with our lives, the ability to read and write in our native language is an asset. Recent studies on the brain show that elementary and high school mathematics, which may have no day-to-day application to anyone but mathematicians and engineers, actually helps to develop our brains in ways that make us better problem solvers as adults.

Another approach to teaching for the future is to key into students' current needs and desires, then trust that teaching to these immediate concerns will instill a philosophy of life-long learning. This is the approach taken by most experiential educators. Rather than trying to predict what basic skills will be useful sometime down the road, the goal is to make learning inherently interesting, so that the students will be motivated to learn the things they need to learn when they need to learn them. Dewey described it as providing experiences that have a certain level of "agreeableness." Worthwhile experiences are enjoyable in themselves, but "are, nevertheless, more than immediately enjoyable since they promote having desirable future experiences."[4]

Teaching to the present, however, does not free educators from having to make educated guesses about what students need. Experiential educators have to determine the immediate needs of students and then teach skills that serve those needs. This is not as easy as it may seem. Most of us, even as adults, have trouble figuring out our learning needs. Younger students, especially children, may not understand or be able to verbalize needs and wants, so it is up to educators to determine what they are. Furthermore, experiential education is student-centered, not student-directed. This means that an experiential educator does not simply determine wants and then cater to them (as, for example, the staff of a vacation resort might cater to the wants and whims of its customers). Instead, an educator uses the intrinsic motivation of immediate wants to draw students to the lessons they need. For example, rock climbing may appeal to the high-thrill mentality of many teenagers, but many climbing instructors are not satisfied with merely facilitating a safe climbing experience. The educator attracts students with rock climbing, but uses the rock climbing instruction to work on self-esteem, trust, cooperation, or an appreciation of the natural world. For example, a student may not know that low self-esteem is a problem or, even if he realizes it, is not likely to ask for help from a teacher. That same student, however, may express an interest in rock climbing, and the educator can facilitate a rock climbing experience to work on what the educator senses is low self-esteem.

This is not to say, however, that there is anything wrong with sometimes making an activity such as rock climbing an end unto itself. While experiential education is laced with metaphors (e.g., rock climbing is a metaphor for facing one's fears, for trusting other people, for completing a task one step at a time), rock climbing can sometimes just be an afternoon of playing on the rocks. Such an activity is a healthy, socially appropriate, life-long leisure pursuit, and that, under some circumstances, is enough. It is possible for the experiential education profession to become overly concerned with turning fun experiences into something "measurably useful." Perhaps because experiential educators are sensitive to criticisms that their activities are diversionary time fillers, they sometimes go too far in putting structure to their programs. One sign of this over planning is mandatory processing, where well-intentioned educators get their students into circles to talk, even when the faces of the students are saying, "Oh no, we're gonna process again."

If intrinsically interesting experiences breed a philosophy of life-long learning, shouldn't that be enough? One concern of an "in its own time" philosophy of teaching is that measurable outcomes may not be readily available. If I teach rock climbing as a way to promote life-long learning, will I be able to measure that my rock climbing course will have instilled a philosophy of experiencing? Probably not, no more than anyone could have predicted that my playing in the woods when I was ten would have anything to do with me studying Chinese when I was forty. This is experiential education's leap of faith. Greta Nagel, in *Tao of Learning*, called it "faith in your students' responsibility for learning."[5] At the same time that experiential educators increasingly use measurable predetermined outcomes to justify their programs, one of their greatest outcomes – that of instilling a philosophy of life-long experiencing and learning – is not something easily measured. Experiential educators just have to trust that it will happen. As Lin Yutang stated it:

> *Our intellectual interests grow like a tree or flow like a river. So long as there is proper sap, the tree will grow anyhow, and so long as there is fresh current from the spring, the water will flow. When water strikes a granite cliff, it just goes around it; when it finds itself in a pleasant low valley, it stops and meanders there a while; when it finds itself in a deep mountain pond it is content to stay there; when it finds itself traveling over rapids, it hurries forward. Thus, without any effort or determined aim, it is sure of reaching the sea some day.[6]*

Perhaps the single most significant thing that experiential education can do is to instill a philosophy of life-long learning in students who do not excel in traditional education. Those who succeed in the traditional classroom are rewarded by the mainstream educational system and therefore enjoy being part of that system; i.e., the successful students come to look on education as a favorable experience and tend to continue, in some fashion, to use the educational opportunities that society offers. While people ought to do what they enjoy even if they are not good at it, the fact is that people are rewarded for the things they do well, and those who are not rewarded tend to stop participating. Poor athletes stop participating in organized sports well before high school. Poor students drop out of school well before graduation – and the educational system too often lets it happen. Instead of finding physical activity that is non-competitive and does not require grace and coordination, poor athletes are allowed to stop exercising. Instead of finding alternative areas of study for students who are falling behind in traditional education, those students either leave school or graduate from high school at the bottom of their class. Even if these students do squeak out a diploma, the humiliation and frustration of repeated failure confirms the notion that formal education is not for them.

This, therefore, provides a valuable niche for experiential education – to teach and introduce success to the students who do not fare well in the traditional setting. Experiential education is no better, nor is it worse, than traditional education – it is just different – so those students who do not find success in one educational methodology might find it in another. Experiential education is an opportunity for students who frequently fail in traditional school to succeed and feel as if the educational system has a place for them.[7]

## PLANTING THE SEED

Making the most of opportunities in the present does not mean that an experiential educator cannot lay some specific groundwork for the students' future. Just because the future is unknown does not mean that a competent instructor does not have a sense of some of things that his or her students will value later in life. However, instead of teaching subjects that have no immediate application to a student's life and trusting that they will be of use in the future, the experiential educator can teach subjects that have immediate relevance and simultaneously plant seeds for the future. These seeds can be as straightforward as announcing to a beginner's yoga class that an intermediate course begins in two weeks. It can be as subtle as taking a group of kids on a hike to an eagle's nest, in part because it might nudge a couple of those kids to become birdwatchers later in life. Many, if not most, of these small hints for future endeavors will never be taken up, but some might take root five or ten years into the future.

When I was a graduate student at the University of Minnesota, I took a course in the pedagogy of higher education. In the course, however, pedagogy rarely was the foremost topic of discussion. Harvey Sarles, the man who was the instructor of the course, was an anthropologist, not a professor of education, and his method of teaching pedagogy was to teach it by example. For the most part, Sarles left it up to the students to determine the topics for the course, and from his guidance in addressing those topics, it was left to the students to derive the pedagogical lessons. One unique thing about the course was that it had no pre-established required reading list. As a group, the students chose a couple of books to read and discuss (*Pedagogy of the Oppressed* was one that I recall), but more often, Sarles would react to something someone had said by getting out of his chair and writing the title of a book on the chalkboard. He'd then follow that by suggesting that we read the book when we thought the time was right. "Plato's *Republic*, you should read that someday." "Wendell Berry's *The Unsettling of America*, you should read Berry sometime before you die."

At the beginning of each class, Professor Sarles would sit quietly in our circle of chairs and wait for a student to start the discussion. One day I started the discussion by saying, "I'm trying to read one of the books that you recommended. It's—*The Image* by Kenneth Boulding. The writing is not difficult, but I'm not getting the point of the book."

When he asked me what I thought the book might be about, I came up with a weak response, and Sarles said, "You're right. You aren't getting the point. But you will. Put the book away and look at it again in a year."

That was the end of the discussion.* No explanation. No tips for deciphering the text. Just instructions to try again when I was

---

* Sarles later explained to the entire class that his decision to not help me understand the book was a conscious decision. If he felt that I was not ready to handle his lack of help, he would have helped. Because he thought I was mature enough to handle the rebuff and then explore *The Image* again when I was ready, he left it to me to understand the book on my own.

ready. It took me five years, not one, to pick up *The Image* again, but now it is one of the most dog-eared books that I own.

I learned two basic lessons from my course with Harvey Sarles. The first lesson, which is one of the most valuable pedagogical lessons I learned in graduate school, is that it is fine to have an area of excellence, but it may be more important to be knowledgeable in a wide range of subjects and skills. Sarles was able to let the students determine the topic of each class, because he had a basic knowledge of just about every topic that came up. Whereas most elements of graduate school were pushing me toward specialization, my developing philosophy of education was doing the opposite. It was becoming evident that students tend to be more interdisciplinary than their teachers, and on this matter, it seemed like the students were right.[8]

The second lesson that I learned from Sarles' course is that education, even education that centers on the current interests of the students, ought to plant seeds. At the same time that an educator should promote a philosophy of experiencing by addressing the current needs and interests of students, he or she might also hint at potential activities down the road. Experiential education opens doors to future experiences, and planting seeds is one way to encourage this.

## WORKING WITH STUDENTS WHERE THEY ARE

If one of experiential education's contributions to education is to help people experience success, then it makes sense that experiential educators develop their programs specifically with this goal in mind. It is not enough to figure out what it is that traditional education unintentionally does that contributes to a sense of failure (e.g., grades, direct comparisons between students, references to winning and losing) and then remove those factors from a program. As Dewey pointed out again and again in *Experience and Education*, it doesn't take any skill to point out some of the problems with traditional education.[9] The hard part is developing a viable alternative.

Unfortunately there is no educational philosophy that succinctly outlines a program for facilitating a feeling of success. The Tao, however, does suggest a couple of general guidelines for leaders who want to promote success in their followers. Neither of the suggestions will surprise a competent experiential educator, but they will confirm some basic tenets of experiential education theory. These guidelines are summarized below.

## USE EACH PERSON'S STRENGTHS

Teaching students at their emotional, physical, and mental levels is a basic principle of experiential education. This is consistent with Tao thinking as well, for the Tao asks that no leader should require followers to perform duties beyond their abilities. There-fore, in order for a leader to assign proper responsibilities, he or she must take the time to assess the strengths and weaknesses of all participants.

The tendency of many experiential educators is to grab student interest quickly by getting to the action portion of the program as soon as possible. While this approach keeps the level of interest high, it may get in the way of initial assessment. Moving immediately to the action part of a program requires that educators either 1) conduct assessment that can be done prior to the program itself or 2) perform on-going informal assessment during the activity and then tweak programming on the spot according to new information about the participants.

In terms of having students experience success, the key to assessment is determining the strengths of each individual. Providing programs that facilitate a feeling of genuine success is difficult, certainly more difficult than facilitating generic programs. It requires that the educator know and understand each student as an individual, not merely a member of a particular group being served. Generic programs may, in fact, work for a group, but not for every individual in that group. For example, a group of students may have accomplished a series of group challenges, but a member of that group did not contribute to the success. The student's lack of coordination or his shyness or his pessimistic attitude actually held the group back, and the student felt as if he was more a part of the obstacle than part of the solution.

Therefore, an effective educator has to determine the strengths of each student and then create learning opportunities that take advantage of those strengths. This is a major theme in the *Huainanzi* and is restated in a number of ways, including those listed below:

> *Horses cannot be used to bear heavy loads; oxen cannot be used to chase the swift... wood cannot be used to make pots. Employ them appropriately, use them where they fit, and all things and all beings are equal as one.*[10]

> *If you focus on people's shortcomings and forget about their strengths, then it will be hard to find worthy people in all the world.*[11]

> *Sages find work for all of them, so no abilities are wasted.*[12]

> *Unprincipled rulers take from the people without measuring the people's strength; they make demands on their subjects without assessing how much their subjects have.*[13]

> *When people are skillfully employed, they are like the legs of a millipede - numerous without interfering with each other. They are like lips and teeth - hard and soft rubbing together without hurting each other.*[14]

## PRAISE AND PUNISH FAIRLY

An inappropriate way to promote a feeling of success is to take conventional programming and merely litter it generously with compliments. This includes saying "good try" when no effort was made or rewarding the entire group when some in the group behaved improperly. Such an approach is similar to a teacher in a traditional setting giving all A's and B's, even when the students did not put forth any effort and did not comprehend the important points of a course. The undeserved good grade boosts a student's grade point average, but any student who feels good about a grade-inflated GPA is buying into a false standard. The unintended lessons of easy grading are 1) everybody can succeed without trying, 2) the goal is the grade and not the learning, and 3) anyone who does put forth effort is a bit of a moron because it really doesn't make any difference anyway.

Passing out undeserved compliments actually is the lazy leader's way to promote success. Instead of discovering the talents of each student and putting them to use, the lazy leader throws out a pre-packaged program and congratulates the participants regardless of the result.

Tao writings are emphatic on the point of rewarding and punishing fairly. The *Wen-tzu*, for example, stated, "When rulers like benevolence, people are rewarded without having achieved anything of worth, and people are allowed to go free even if they have committed crimes. When rulers like punishment, worthy people are neglected."[15] Conveying the same thought, Liu I-ming writes, "Benevolence is the soft path, based on compassion and love. Duty is the hard path, based on judgment and administration. If one is only benevolent, without duty, then love will lack distinction of right and wrong. If one is dutiful without benevolence, then judgment will become oppressive. Both of these states miss the center."[16] The *Huainanzi*, which among Taoist writings is noted for its explicitness, is very explicit when it comes to reward and punishment. It goes so far as to assert that rewarding fairly is, along with feeding the hungry and allowing the weary to rest, one of the three basic things that people want from their rulers.[17] The *Huainanzi* also states, "If rich rewards are given to those without merit, and high titles are given to those who have not worked, then people in office will be lazy about their duties, and idlers will advance rapidly."[18]

## CONCLUSION

In "Birdwatching at Fifty," the story that opened this chapter, a college student says that something as boring as birdwatching should be relegated to people who are fifty years old. Such a statement is in strong contrast to Plato's claim that a leader should be fifty before he is allowed to govern[19] and Confucius' assertion that a person must live for fifty years before he or she is ready to read the *I Ching*.[20] In the birdwatching story, a half century of living is equated with reaching old age and giving up on new and exciting experiences. In the philosophy of the old masters, fifty years represents the amount of time needed to prepare for the most complex experiences yet to come.

These two images of middle age actually provide an interesting way for experiential educators to evaluate their teaching. When working with students, at least with students who themselves have not reached fifty years of age, which reality of fifty are the educator's learning experiences helping to create? There is nothing wrong with people slowing down after years of raising a family and establishing a career (in fact, most of us should have been going slower in the first place), but a philosophy of lifelong learning should be lifelong – especially if, as Plato and Confucius suggest, the experiences have the potential of being progressively more interesting.

The Iroquois people have the tradition of the Seventh Generation.[21] This concept requires that in all deliberations, leaders ask themselves how their actions today will affect descendents for the next seven generations. Even though the actions are done to satisfy immediate needs, there is a realization that in acting for the present there is an impact on the future. In the same spirit as seventh generation thinking – that is working for present concerns, but looking out for the future – educators might evaluate their programs by asking, "How will educational programs designed to serve students' current needs affect those students when they are fifty?"

# SECTION THREE
## The Role of Nature

embrace
nature

One of the reasons for the popularity of Tao philosophy in the West is the Tao's respect for the natural world. Predominant Western perspectives, especially Judeo-Christian theology, has until recently either ignored or subordinated the non-human, so as people sensed for themselves a spiritual or mystical connection to nature, they turned to Buddhism, Native American thinking, and Taoism for their philosophical foundation. Taoism was especially appealing, because it is not romantic communion with the plants and the animals, but recognition that everyday life is closely linked to nature. As Alan Watts put it, "the Taoist idea of naturalness goes far beyond the merely normal, or the simply unostentatious way of behaving. It is the concrete realization that all our experiences and actions are movements of the Tao, the way of nature, the endless knot, including the very experience of being an individual, a knowing subject."[1] With this perspective, Tao thinking has much in common with American Transcendentalism, and Thoreau and Emerson will be cited as often as Lao-tzu and Chuangtze in the chapters that follow. Section Three looks at the Tao perspective on the nature-human relationship and applies it to experiential education. While all three chapters in this section advocate spending time in natural places, it is more than merely going into nature. It is going into nature with an open frame of mind.

endlessness

cleanse
the mind

EMBRACE NATURE

# 10

## The Inventor's Mantle Clock

On the table between the Leader Who Is Hardly Known and the inventor sat an old mantle clock. The face and the hands of the clock were missing, and in their place was an illuminated photograph of the moon. Somehow within the workings of the clock a shadow was cast on the photograph, and nearly half of the moon was in darkness.

"This," said the inventor, "is my latest creation. It is a clock, but it does not tell normal time. Instead this clock keeps track of the phases of the moon."

"May I pick it up to look more closely?" asked the Leader Who Is Hardly Known.

"Of course!" exclaimed the inventor. "I respect your opinion. I only show you my creations to get your assessment as to their worth."

After he brought the clock up to his face, the Leader Who Is Hardly Known asked, "Do you mean that you have developed a mechanism so slow that one revolution is twenty-eight days instead of an hour—and that the moon in your clock is a half moon because the real moon also is waxing toward full?"

"Yes," said the inventor. "Cycles are very trendy, and my clock will help people keep track of the lunar cycle."

"You mean that you expect people to buy your clock instead of stepping outside for a few seconds to look up into the sky?"

"That's right, because people don't look at the moon. And even if they do, they don't have any idea whether a half moon is moving toward full or away from it. The clock would tell them that."

"But the waxing and waning of the moon are shown on many calendars. I do not think this is one of your best ideas."

"You are the great naturalist," said the inventor, "but sometimes I think you spend too much time in the woods. If you want people to connect more with nature, then you have to provide incentives and bookmarks for them to do so. This clock also is an alarm clock, and the alarm only goes off on the full moon. Right now the alarm plays "Moon River," but I think I need something better. Anyway, my clock tells people it is time to go outside and look at the full moon. Build it and they will go."

"I think," responded the Leader Who is Hardly Known, "that it is impossible to spend too much time in the woods, but you make a very good point. I know the phases of the moon without your clock, but only because it is important to my work. The brightness of the night determines where I go for my night hikes. When the moon is new and the night is dark, I stay to the open fields. When the moon is full and it shines as brightly as a light to read by, I can take the children into the forest."

"Then you are a lucky man," said the inventor, "and my respect for your work has just increased significantly. It had not occurred to me that anyone other than cat burglars and lovers paid any attention to the moon. You are a person whose life is touched by the rhythms of nature."

"You are right, but I had not thought of it that way before. I knew that I was fortunate to have enjoyable work, but it hadn't occurred to me that work that brings a person closer to nature is such a rarity – so much so that others need an alarm clock to remind them that nature is even there.

"Thank you," continued the Leader Who is Hardly Known. "You and your not-so-silly clock have taught me a valuable lesson.

Most people no longer have practical day-to-day reasons for understanding the patterns and cycles of nature. Therefore, it must be the job of the experiential educator to provide those reasons."

## IN NATURE WE SEE OURSELVES

*Respect for the unknown is the attitude of those who, instead of raping nature, woo her until she gives herself. But what she gives, even then, is not the cold clarity of the surface but the warm inwardness of the body.*[1]

Alan Watts

The essay that follows is not the one that I had expected to write. Because I am concerned that some experiential educators are moving their programs away from natural areas and abdicating their environmental responsibilities, I was ready to moralize about experiential education's obligation to help protect the earth. Yet when I carefully studied the Taoist perspective on the nature-human relationship, I realized that the theme coming through strongest and loudest was not a message of tree-hugging preservation. Instead I found a more sophisticated and a more humanistic perspective, and interestingly, a lesson more central to experiential education theory.

### THE TAOIST PERSPECTIVE ON THE NATURE-HUMAN RELATIONSHIP

According to Tao writings, humanity is not part of the natural world, but it is not separate from her either. Nature and humanity are actually polarities or complementary opposites. While neither was specifically created for the other, each depends upon the other for its well-being. As Alan Watts described it, humanity and nature are not the same, but are of the same process.[2]

Ecologically speaking, the nature-human relationship is a symbiosis. Tao-ically speaking, it is the yin and the yang. If, however, it is a symbiotic relationship, what does nature get out of the deal? Humans obviously benefit from their ties with the natural world, but does nature really gain? One answer to that question, although one that may not be satisfactory from a biocentric point of view, is that humanity completes nature. It takes the human mind to identify the links between nature and humankind, and in doing so, consciously builds the relationship between the two. As Cheng Chung-ying describes it:

> *Chinese philosophy focuses on man as the consummator of nature rather than man as the conqueror of nature, as a participant in nature rather than a predator of nature. Man as the consummator of nature expresses continuously the beauty, truth, and goodness of nature; and articulates them in a moral or natural cultivation of human life or human nature...*[3]

An immediate response to this viewpoint might be that nature would be better off without the connections. That, however, is not true. The problem with the nature-human relationship is the way some humans use the connections, not the connections themselves. In fact, the most detestable actions against nature have occurred by those humans who do not acknowledge the existence of connections. To say that nature would be better off without humans because of mistreatment is analogous to saying that recent immigrants to the United States would be better off without the American-born population. The solution is to change the mistreatment of immigrants, not sever the ties.

The best way to change the action is to realize that the beauty, truth, and goodness of nature are actually a manifestation of the Tao. A person who is wise enough to transfer those attributes into his or her own life then is a person living the Tao. According to the *Tao Te Ching*, "Man follows the ways of Earth, Earth follows the ways of Heaven, and Heaven follows the Tao."[4] This passage suggests there are more than environmental ethics lost when programs are taken out of the natural setting. The more human-centered goals of experiential education also are sacrificed. There is a fallacy in assuming that team-building and self-esteem, peace education and justice, emotional health and addiction treatment do not suffer when an agency pulls programs out of natural areas. While it may be stating the obvious, ropes courses, gymnasiums, and meeting rooms are not the same as the natural world.

## ARE EXPERIENTIAL EDUCATORS USING NATURAL AREAS LESS?

The Tao relationship with nature says that not only does humanity require nature as the source of food, natural resources, and recreation, but also to be self-actualized humans. If this is so, then why does it seem that some experiential educators have made less, not more use of nature in their programming? I do not know whether the headcount of people being led into natural areas by experiential educators has gone up or down over the past twenty years. Regardless, there are two things that have happened to reduce the impact that nature can make on individuals. One is that, in many instances, the length of stay in nature has shortened. The prime example is the school classroom that once went to nature camp for a week and now spends a day at the local nature center. The second is that many experiential education organizations have gradually shifted their programs from natural places to human-made facilities.

There are a couple of good reasons why natural areas are being used less by some agencies. A big one is the popularity of ropes and challenges courses. Ropes courses can take the adventure of wilderness experiences out of the wilderness and bring it to where the people are. These courses are a convenient and safe way to accomplish some of the self-esteem and group cohesion goals that before were taught in the backcountry. In some ways, ropes courses are even better teaching environments than pristine nature, because many of the uncertainties of backcountry travel are greatly reduced. On a ropes course, weather changes, the physical stamina of participants, access to medical facilities, etc... are not the worrisome variables they are when a group is two or three days from civilization. In comparison to a backcountry canoe or backpacking trip, ropes and challenge courses are quick and safe alternatives.

As such, ropes courses are an excellent addition to the experiential education repertoire. They have afforded adventure experiences to many people who could not or would not go on a wilderness trip. Still they are not nature. Some organizations have gone exclusively to ropes courses as their adventure component, even taking the same clients through a ropes course experience on an annual, monthly, even weekly basis. Ropes courses, when used most effectively, are a companion or a prelude to nature-based adventure. If at all possible, they should not be a substitute.

Another reason that natural areas are being used less than they could be are the restrictions of time and money. Two of the first questions any potential client asks an experiential educator when considering a program is "how much does this cost?" and "how long does it take?" Many organizations that use experiential education programs as a therapeutic tool never did have a lot of money, and now with insurance companies and social service agencies restricting the length of a stay for a patient or client, some do not even have the time for an extended outdoor adventure. Corporate groups, while often able to afford the extended trip, are not willing to give up the time for a training program that has less than clear-cut outcomes. Ironically, with the high cost of incarceration and the political demand for longer sentencing, those in criminal detention are the client group with the money and time for an extended outdoor experience. "Go-to-camp-or-go-to-jail" programs for juvenile offenders may be the experiential education component getting the most time in natural settings. Fortunately, in communities where prevention is a high priority, at-risk youth may be the trickle down beneficiaries of this trend.

## NATURE AS METAPHOR

The Tao perspective on the nature-human relationship has much in common with the American Transcendentalists, especially Ralph Waldo Emerson. In his essay, *Nature*, Emerson echoed Lao-tzu when he wrote that people can understand themselves only by spending time in nature:

*Every appearance in nature corresponds to some state of the mind, and that state of the mind can only be described by presenting that natural appearance as its picture.... All the facts in natural history taken by themselves, have no value, but are barren like a single sex. But marry it to human history, and it is full of life.... We are thus assisted by natural objects in the expression of particular meanings. But how great a language to convey such peppercorn informations!....The world is emblematic. Parts of speech are metaphors because the whole of nature is a metaphor of the human mind.[5]*

If there is a word that should catch the attention of an experiential educator, it is "metaphor." Metaphors have been a standard in experiential education methodology since the early 1980s.[6] The basic experiential education mechanism for transferring the lessons of an activity to everyday life is the use of metaphors. For example, asking for help on a high ropes element is a metaphor for asking for help in a personal fight against alcoholism. Males automatically taking the leadership roles in a co-educational group initiative is a metaphor for gender issues in the workplace. Minimum impact in the back country is a metaphor for respect and care of a person's neighborhood back home.

Direct interaction with nature minimizes the intervention of the facilitator and lessens the chances for corrupted messages. On this matter, Roger Ames recommends "deferring to the integrity of the environment."[7] For example, a group of corporate executives going through a one-day ropes and challenge course could reasonably conclude that the lesson of the day is "Cooperation between departments leads to increased profits." The same group on a week-long wilderness canoe trip might come to the same conclusion, but they might also realize that employee well-being and environmental compliance are just as important as money in the success of a business.

If the lessons of nature show individuals how to live their lives, then direct contact with nature should be encouraged with virtually any program. Should a children's museum only three blocks from a river have a river exhibit? If the exhibit is the enticement for children to go the river, the exhibit serves a purpose. If the exhibit is a substitute for going to the river, the exhibit is an obstacle to experience. If an indoor climbing wall is the first step to going to the mountain, the climbing wall serves a purpose. If that wall is a convenient way to get the thrill of the mountain without the hassle of travel and set up, then the educative value of the climbing wall is much less than what it could be.

I know of a well-intentioned recreation resource manager who went to great expense to build a 360° theatre at the visitor center of a national park in order to show the natural wonders of the place. Now many people go to the park only to see the movie.

## CONCLUSION

The Tao definition of humankind's relationship with nature makes a much stronger argument for nature education in experiential education than I had originally imagined. The argument is not that experiential education needs to teach environmentally so that students develop an environmental ethic. It is that humans need to take care of themselves, and the way to do that is to understand nature. Nature adheres to the Tao. Humans need to adhere to the Tao to be healthy. The way to understand the Tao is to understand nature.

This perspective actually addresses my concern with experiential education much better than an avid environmentalism perspective might. A biocentric view such as Deep Ecology says that the rivers, the mountains, the plants and animals all have an innate right to exist. The Tao perspective is much more anthropocentric or people-oriented. It does not say that all experiential educators need to add environmental awareness to their mission. It says that an understanding of nature will address an experiential educator's mission, even if that mission is not environmentally oriented. Nature does have an innate right to exist, but an effective tool in preserving that right is to show people that their own mental well-being depends on nature's existence.

Can a person find the Tao without understanding, appreciating, and being in nature? This question is like asking whether the world would still be wonderful without the laughter of children, good books, and rock n' roll. Certainly Lin Yutang has an opinion on the matter, for he tells a story of a man who asks God for a new planet, because this one is not good enough. God points out distant hills and the sky and the petals of an orchid and asks if this is not worthy of any human. The man says that they are common and ordinary. God reveals to him colorful fish, cool breezes, and the sound of wind through pine forests, and the man says that these things mean nothing to him. God takes him to the Grand Canyon, the Himalayas, and the cliffs of the Yangtse Gorges, and the man says that this planet still offers nothing worthwhile. God eventually loses his temper and responds, "I will send you to Hell where you shall not see the sailing clouds and the flowering trees, nor hear the gurgling brooks and live there forever till the end of your days." Then God sends him to live in an apartment in the city.[8]

無

極

ENDLESSNESS

# 11

# The Interrupted Stargazers

The Leader Who is Hardly Known went backpacking with Ed, an old friend from California, during the last week of May. They were hiking along the edge of a shallow lake, when a pair of Canada geese darted across the trail and jumped into the lake. The two birds frantically swam toward open water, honking the entire way.

"Look carefully," said Ed. "I'm pretty sure those geese are distracting us from their young."

The friend, however, need not have made the warning, for as he said it, the goslings blew their cover. From the same spot where the adult geese had dashed out of the high grass, three baby geese panicked and they too shot across the trail and jumped into the water. The young birds swam no more than ten feet, then disappeared under the surface of the lake.

"That's impossible," exclaimed Ed. "Geese can't dive!"

"Obviously they can," responded the Leader Who is Hardly Known. "One of the reasons I enjoy these trips with you is your knowledge of natural history. I learn many things each time we go out together. It is important, however, that your knowledge expands, rather than narrows, your observation skills. And when your senses contradict that knowledge, do not be quick to assume it is your senses that are wrong. At this moment, I know that geese, at least baby ones, can dive beneath the surface of the water, and no prior knowledge will shake me from that realization."

The two backpackers continued down the trail for another two hours and then set up camp just inside the forest next to a large meadow. They ate a simple meal and finished dinner clean-up right at dusk, so Ed suggested that they lie down in the meadow and watch the stars come out. "With no clouds and no city lights for miles, the night sky should be exceptional."

"That's an excellent idea," said the Leader Who is Hardly Known. "It is when we watch for no reason other than the pleasure of watching that nature reveals herself."

The early evening air was quickly getting cold, so the Leader Who is Hardly Known and his friend carried their sleeping pads and sleeping bags into the meadow. They stretched out on their pads and covered themselves with their bags so only their heads stuck out. At first the two talked about the geese and the other high-lights of the day, but soon fell quiet as the first evening stars started to show themselves in the darkening sky. The two were content, silent, and motionless bodies alone in the wilderness.

Suddenly, from nowhere, a great horned owl materialized only feet above the face of the Leader Who is Hardly Known. With wings spread and talons drawn, the bird dominated his field of vision. Instinctively both men threw up their arms and buried their faces into the nylon and down of their sleeping bags. Seconds later, they looked out, but, of course, the owl was gone.

"Damn," cried Ed. "it would have clawed your eyes out! It must have thought your head was a rabbit or something."

"That was wonderful," exclaimed the Leader Who is Hardly Known. "We were one with nature, and there was no distinction between the seer and the seen."

 HOW TO SEE NATURE

*There is another kind of seeing that involves a letting go.*[1]
Annie Dillard

"Untrammeled" is a word I have seen in print only twice. It means "not subject to the human controls and manipulations that hamper the free play of natural forces."[2] The first time I saw untrammeled was in its most renown use, as part of the 1964 Wilderness Act. Section 2 of the Act offers a colorful description of the land that the law is intended to protect. It defines wilderness as "an area where the earth and its community of life are untrammeled by man, where man himself is a visitor who does not remain."[3] The second time I saw untrammeled was in a translation of the ancient Taoist work *Wen-tzu*. Here the passage read, "Emptiness means there is no burden within. Evenness means the mind is untrammeled." [4]

When I saw "untrammeled" in the Wilderness Act, I was impressed. (First, I had to look it up in the dictionary, but then I was impressed.) The federal government of the United States was going to protect large selected tracts of land to the extent that natural processes would not be affected by human influences. So long as the law was enforced, there would always be places to go where there would be no roads, no buildings, nothing that would prevent someone from seeing nature in its purest form. Yet as evocative as untrammeled's use is in the Wilderness Act, it is more so in the *Wen-tzu*. Here ancient Chinese writing—or at least Thomas Cleary's English interpretation of the writing—says that the mind can be untrammeled. The mind, that part of us that is the most distinctly human, might be so open and so empty as to not be subject to human controls. Furthermore, because the word "untrammeled" is associated with the Wilderness Act, it also connotes a wilderness. I am not exactly sure what it means to have a mind that is a wilderness, but I do know that is something I want to know more about. I am certainly intrigued with the notion of meeting pristine nature with a pristine mind.

## LEAVE THE CLUTTER BEHIND

Tao writings teach that people must experience nature if they hope to understand their Tao selves. Experiencing nature, however, is much more than spending time in a natural setting. There certainly are times that all of us go to a natural area, but carry along the problems of everyday life. We walk in the woods or along the shore, but our minds are back at work or back at home. The surroundings serve no more than a pretty place to worry or plan or reflect on something other than nature. Experiential education sometimes takes this preoccupation with everyday problems even another step in that it *intentionally* opens up this mental baggage, using natural areas not as a place to experience nature, but as a unique setting from which to work on self-esteem, team-building, even ways to enhance corporate profitability. The paradox, at least from the perspective of the Tao, is that we might learn more about ourselves by truly experiencing nature than by simply using nature as a backdrop for our therapeutic or corporate programming. Rather than looking at nature through a haze of other concerns, it might be better to experience nature with an open and empty mind. There should be no predetermined purpose, no mental distractions, no expectations. Alan Watts, in *Nature, Man and Woman*, describes this frame of mind as a heron hunting in a marsh:

> ... a heron stands stock-still at the edge of a pool, gazing into the water. It does not seem to be looking for fish, and yet the moment a fish moves it dives. (The way to see nature) is, then, simply to observe silently, openly, and without seeking any particular result. It signifies a mode of observation in which there is no duality of seer and seen: there is simply the seeing.[5]

As a ten-year-old kid, I remember trout fishing directly across the river from an otter that was also fishing. The otter came; I fished. The otter fished; I still fished. The otter left, and I kept on fishing. I liked it that the otter was there and unbothered by my presence, but its appearance was simply observed and enjoyed. If I recall correctly, I did not even mention it to my dad when we got back together to drive home from the trout stream. I was too young to realize that having an otter as a fishing companion was a once-in-a-lifetime experience, so it was no big deal. Spending quiet time with nature was just something good to do, as good as playing baseball, better than going to school or doing the dishes, but nothing treasured as a rarity. It was just one of many interesting things that I did.

Unfortunately my pre-teen years were the last time an open relationship with nature came so spontaneously. Now, as an adult, the same kind of experience has to be consciously arranged. No, that is the wrong phrase. It sounds too calculating. Now the same kind of experience needs practice.

So what can be done to help the cluttered adult mind meet nature with an open, free, and empty attitude? I know of two things that will help. First of all, a person must mentally leave the normal daily concerns and thoughts back at the trailhead. Too often people get their bodies into a natural area, but leave their minds somewhere else. For me, it takes a night or two in my backpacking tent before I sleep well. I realize that part of the problem is re-acclimation to mummy bags and hard ground, but a bigger reason is the time it takes for the worries of work and home to peel away.

Second, meeting nature with an open and untrammeled mind requires that a person not clear out the mental closet only to fill it up with something else — even something as productive as outdoor living skills, therapeutic counseling, group dynamics training, or biological/geological/historical information.

This second claim, I realize, runs contrary to experiential education methodology. Teaching outdoor living skills, conducting therapy sessions, facilitating team-building initiatives, and teaching natural and cultural history are what experiential educators do. These are basic reasons that experiential educators take groups into natural areas in the first place. Still this does not negate the fact that these planned activities are impediments to spontaneously encountering nature with an open mind. It is analogous to the girl on an organized nature hike who is reprimanded for cloud gazing when the topic of the day is pond study.

Experiential education has long looked at nature as a classroom. This image is useful, but it receives more credence than it deserves. Experiential educators sometimes pat themselves on the back for getting students into natural areas, but getting them there just to use nature as a backdrop is not enough. Nature is much more than a classroom. It is also the teacher.

## Quiet Watching and Walking Meditation

Obviously experiential education is not going to, nor should it, abandon many of its reasons for being. However, it needs to acknowledge that most programs do not come near to using nature to its full educational potential. Students, in addition to the normal experiential education fare they receive, ought to learn to encounter nature with an open mind. It is not an exaggeration to say that to do anything less can mean that the most important lessons may go unlearned.

Without sacrificing the other programming, there are a few very basic exercises that experiential educators might include when they have a group for an extended time in natural areas. I want to mention two of them here. One is called quiet watching. The other is walking meditation.

LESSON: It is not enough to get people to natural areas. They must also be trained to have open minds. Two simple techniques to promote an openness toward nature are quiet watching and walking meditation.

QUIET WATCHING is no more than the meditation technique of quietly watching an object for an extended period of time (10 minutes or more). The key is to keep the mind focused on the object being watched. When thoughts drift to something else (e.g., the job, family issues, what's for dinner), the meditator realizes she has momentarily lost her focus and gently returns her attention back to the object. Taoist teacher Hua-Ching Ni recommends using large objects of nature as the points of meditation; clouds, a mountain, the tide, a pond.[6] He also thinks that campfires are an excellent point of focus, a fact well known to the thousands of experiential educators who have lost themselves in the flickers of the evening campfire.

The following is Ni's suggestion for watching still another recommended point of focus, a waterfall:

> Sometimes emotions can be destructive to oneself or to one's environment: nature is the cure. Go to a place with a big wa-

*terfall and sit near the bottom, but not where you will get wet. By looking at the waterfall coming down from the sky, you will be washed and cleansed by it. Your emotions and your psychological experiences will be washed away. The water comes from the highness of the mountain; it rushes down to hit the pond or stones beneath it, pounding through the obstacle in your life. Through perseverance, a stone gives way and is shaped by water. Also, by the action of the water, a pond is formed. Use the waterfall to cleanse away your worries, the contamination from your experiences in the world, and your disappointed thoughts about something that has failed or something that cannot come.[7]*

Lin Yutang, in addition to quiet watching, suggests WALKING MEDITATION, "a different kind of travel, travel to see nothing and to see nobody, but the squirrels and muskrats and woodchucks and clouds and trees."[8] He tells the story of an American woman who joined some Chinese friends for a morning walk up a mountain. There was a heavy mist and really nothing to see except fog. The woman immediately wanted to turn back to her warm living quarters, but her friends insisted that she come to see the wondrous sights. Part way up the mountain, her friends became excited about coming across one of the highlights of the mountain. The woman saw only an ugly rock shrouded in clouds, but her friends told her that it was the Inverted Lotus. The woman was cold and wet and disappointed, and she wanted to head back down the mountain. Again her friends insisted that she continue, for the best was at the top of the mountain. When the small group reached the summit, mist and fog were all around them, and all that could be seen was the faint outlines of the surrounding mountains. "There is nothing to see," the woman protested. "Yes," said her Chinese friends, "that is the point. We come up here to see nothing."[9]

A goal of walking meditation, in this case, is not inner enlightenment, as delightful as that would be. It is openness. Stated another way, it is to develop the rare skill of sauntering. Sauntering is roving and wandering with a purpose, but having that purpose be the pleasure of roving and wandering. Henry David Thoreau, in his essay Walking, claimed that the word saunterer derived from vagabonds during the Middle Ages who claimed that they were going "a la Sainte Terre," to the Holy Land. When one of these people wandered into a town asking for charity, the children would call him a "Sainte Terrer." The key, according to Thoreau, is to totally unload the worries and obligations of civilization, then walk into the woods both bodily and in spirit. Only then can it be said that "every walk is a sort of crusade."[10]

## THE WALKABOUT

For those readers who think that quiet watching or walking meditation is too woo-woo* for their tastes, I would like to describe a one-credit course that I offer at my university each May. I mention it because it incorporates the sentiments of seeing nature with an open mind. It is an attempt to introduce "slow walking" to twenty-year-old university students who generally seek more action in their nature encounters. The course content, however, contains nothing that even the most straight-laced student would interpret as Taoist mumbo jumbo.

The class is called the walkabout.** Up to a dozen students and I travel an hour and half from the University of Wisconsin-La Crosse campus to spend 24 hours in a relatively remote section of the Black River State Forest. The State Forest is a mix of marsh, small forest, and pine/oak barrens. The marshy areas just outside of the Forest's boundaries have been diked to create the largest cranberry industry in the United States. Some of the marshes in the Forest have also been diked, in this case to establish waterfowl habitat. The stated purpose of the walkabout is no more than to carefully and quietly observe nature for one full day.

The course attracts an odd group of students, only a small minority of them enrolled because they want to spend quiet time with nature. That is because of the unusual timing and design of the

---

*"Woo-woo" is a term used by some traditional environmentalists to describe New Age environmentalists who go to nature largely for its spiritual and/or supernatural qualities. When people use the term, it usually is slightly derogatory; they are intrigued, but the subject matter is a little too weird for their taste.

course. First of all, the course is quick; there are three pre-trip meetings and the 24-hour excursion. The whole course takes only five days. Also the course occurs the week immediately following spring semester exams. As a result I get students who need only one more credit for a minor in Recreation Management, students who want to knock off a quick credit before starting their summer jobs, and students who thought that they were going to graduate in the spring, but because of some foul-up, find themselves one credit short of graduation. Mixed in with this group are the few outdoor recreation enthusiasts hungry for anything that will get them into the field at this very traditional university. The point to be made here is that the class is not anything like preaching to the choir. A better description would be, "I don't want to do this, but it's only for 24 hours."

The three pre-trip meetings have three distinct purposes. The first day, ice breakers and group initiatives help people get to know each other. The second meeting is map and compass training, the only outdoor living skill taught in the entire course. This is included because the students might do a bit of wandering on their own during the walkabout. The third meeting is a short hike up a nearby scenic bluff. At the top of the bluff, members of the group take turns reading passages from Thoreau, Aldo Leopold, Annie Dillard, and John Muir about enjoying nature in a quiet and peaceful manner.

The course, except for the map and compass, is not an outdoor living class. There is no cooking. Each person is given a 24-hour supply of gorp, fruit, and pita bread and eats whenever he or she wants to. There is one cookstove to make hot drinks at night around the campfire and then again in the morning, but the leader operates it. There isn't even tent setup, as pairs or trios of students are given tarp and rope and asked to build whatever shelter they feel like. Some opt for no shelter at all and use their tarp as a ground cloth.

---

**I realize that this is misuse of the term associated with the Australian walkabout. I hope that readers can overlook the political incorrectness here to see the value of the course.

The purpose of the course is interaction with nature. No field instruction, no environmental education. The only requirements are that the students be upbeat and open to noticing the things around them. There is a portable library of wildlife identification guides (birds, flowers, bugs, trees) and nature writers, but students only dig into them if they want to.

The walkabout is Friday noon to Saturday noon. There are three planned walks in the 24-hour period. All are optional. The first is Friday afternoon and is the ascent of Wildcat Mountain. For those not familiar with the state of Wisconsin, I should point out that there are no mountains in Wisconsin. We use the term loosely. For any American outside of the Midwest or Florida, this would more accurately be described as the ascent of Wildcat Hill.*** The Wildcat Mountain trip is map and compass practice, a follow-up lesson to the instruction given back at campus. The students, as a group, are given a starting point and a destination, and with the instructor in tow, must get from camp to the mountain and back.

Base camp is adjacent to a diked area, a checkerboard of levees and duck ponds. It is an excellent place to let novice students wander on their own, for they can wind around on the levees for a couple of hours and still have visual sight of camp. Late Friday afternoon is free time. Students are encouraged to go for short walks or relax in camp. I go for a levee walk myself, and any of the students are welcome to come along.

The second planned hike is the night hike, also out on the diked trails adjacent to camp. To hike into the middle of the huge open area is spectacular, as it provides a 360° panorama for stargazing. The last hike is on Saturday morning, and it is a mile and a half solo walk back to the van. The trail chosen is through the woods. The route has no intersections with other trails, so as long as stu-

---

*** As long as I am commenting on the name of Wildcat Mountain, I could also mention that I have, in over a dozen visits, never seen evidence of bobcats (although I believe that they live there). The place has, however, allowed students to see many animals for the first time. These have included sandhill cranes, oppossums, porcupines, and skunks. I, having grown up in the Badger State, saw my first badger there.

dents stay on the trail, they cannot get lost, and eventually they will end up in the parking lot.

## To Process or Not Process

My own experiential education training has made me a believer in processing. Too often the specific lessons of an activity are not obvious to the students, and it is important to talk students past their cliché notions of cooperation, self-esteem, and the beauty of nature. On the walkabout, however, I consciously fight my own inclinations to process each experience.

Usually experiential education is action followed by reflection through processing. The walkabout is unique in that the experience itself is reflective, so it would seem that formal processing would be somewhat redundant. It would be reflecting on the reflection. Therefore formal processing is reduced. Students are given small pocket journals and encouraged to record their thoughts. Twice during the 24 hours, the group gets together in a formal processing circle. The first is prior to the night hike, and the other is just prior to the solo walk (it originally was after the solo walk, but once at the vans, the students' minds were already heading back to their everyday lives).

In most instances, processing discussions narrow in on two things – one is surprise at how quickly the initial fear and distaste of insects and ticks become simply a nuisance, and two is a sincere appreciation at being coerced into slowing down in a natural area. Most students cannot remember the last time that they have truly slowed down. Even their vacations tend to be constant action, and it took a course requirement of relaxation and quiet observation to remind them that periods of reflection are valuable. Some say that one day is not long enough, others claim that they want to get their boyfriend or girlfriend and return the following weekend, still others admit that, while good, it will be a long time before they do another walkabout on their own.

## Conclusion

Let me conclude with a quote from Alan Watts in *Taoism Way Beyond Seeking*. The passage is about Asian art, specifically the classic Chinese and Japanese landscapes of sheer vertical mountains and tumbling mountain streams. In Watts' attempt to explain the art, he introduces the Japanese concept of "yugen," which can roughly be defined as a subtle and mysterious glimpse into the beauty of the eternal. Watts writes not so much to the art's aesthetic value as to the message for the saunterer.

> *A favorite scene is of a mountain landscape, with a tiny little human figure in it somewhere, a poet wandering through pine trees beside a stream. Where is he going? Where is the stream going? Where are the clouds going? Where are the birds going? We don't know, really. They are wandering on. And so, within this idea of wandering you can discover the quality that the Japanese call yugen. Yugen is made up of two characters that mean "mysterious" and "deep." In Japanese poetry yugen is what you feel when you watch wild geese and they are suddenly hidden by a cloud. It is what you feel when you are looking at ships far out to sea and they slowly sail behind a far off island. Yugen is to wander on and on in a great forest without thought of return.*[11]

CLEANSE THE MIND

# 12

# The Owl and the Lady's Slipper

The Leader Who is Hardly Known had signed up for a series of weekend ornithology workshops at a local nature center, and on this particular weekend the topic was owls. The workshop began with a classroom session of dissecting barred owl pellets, and the class had fun in a clumsy attempt to reconstruct a mouse skeleton from its bone collection. Owl pellets are small balls of hair, feathers, and bones that owls regurgitate as part of the digestive process.

After the owl pellet exercise, the instructor took the class out into the nature center's reserve to actually search for owl pellets. The best way to find owl pellets is to look for a high concentration of bird droppings under a tree or shrub. The droppings might mark the location of an owl roost, and where the owl roosts is also where it coughs up pellets. The class split into pairs to search a wide area, and the Leader Who is Hardly Known and his partner found drop-pings under a small stand of chokecherry on the edge of an open field. Big owls, like the barred and great horned, usually rest high in trees, but the small ones commonly roost in shrubbery. Working on her hands and knees, the partner found an owl pellet and immedi-ately intensified her search, now confident that they were under the roost of a saw-whet or screech owl. With her face buried in the tall grass beneath the thicket, the Leader Who is Hardly Known quietly tapped her on the shoulder. When she looked up, he pointed to a spot two feet in front of her face. There, staring back at the woman, was a saw-whet owl. She had been so intent on finding owl pellets that she'd failed to see the small bird that had coughed them up.

Both the woman and the Leader Who is Hardly Known watched the owl for about ten minutes, then gathered the rest of the class to show them the bird. Afterwards the partner spoke to the Leader

Who is Hardly Known. "I feel a little stupid that I didn't see the owl when it was close enough to bite me on the nose. If my four-year daughter saw bird poop all over the ground, she'd know enough to look for the bird that made it. I'm the birder in the family, and it didn't even occur to me that the owl would be in its roost."

The Leader Who is Hardly Known responded, "Oh, I would expect a four-year old child to be more observant than either you or me. Your daughter still sees with an open mind, whereas our brains are so cluttered that it limits our vision. Today your mind was focused on owl pellets, so owl pellets were all you were going to find."

"But you noticed the owl," the woman said. "We had the same assignment. I buried my head in the grass, and you looked for the owl."

"That is because nature has already given me the lesson that you learned only today. Many years ago I stepped on a yellow lady's slipper while I was birdwatching. I had been looking up, so I noticed the delicate flower only after my foot came down on it. I tried to prop the flower back up, but it was crushed too badly to be saved. I felt guilty that my inattentiveness – actually my over-attentiveness to one thing at the expense of another – caused damage to the flower. As a result, now when I enter a natural area, especially when I go there with a specific purpose in mind, I quickly think about lady's slippers before I go in. It is a reminder to keep an empty mind, for that is when the beautiful discoveries are made.

"So consider yourself lucky," the Leader Who is Hardly Known continued. "You now have your own reminder. Some people think owls represent wisdom or silence or the dangers of the night, but for you, owls are a metaphor for an open and empty mind."

## NATURE'S LESSONS

*The ears of someone whose eyes are examining the tip of a*
*fine hair do not hear the peal of thunder; the eyes of someone*

*whose ears are tuning a musical instruction do not see enor-*
*mous mountains. Thus when there is fixation of attention on*
*small things, then there is forgetfulness of great things.*[1]

From the Went-zu

Experiential educators who recognize nature as a teacher learn lessons for living from their experiences in the natural world. Because most of these lessons are discovered independent of any
formal instruction, a reasonable question is, "Do experiential educators share their lessons with students, or do they trust that the
students will find lessons on their own?"

The answer to the question is that sharing lessons and having
trust in student self-discovery are not mutually exclusive, and an
educator needs to do both. An effective leader can share a lesson
with students when that lesson relates well to the moment and
still believe that the lesson will prod students to discover other lessons on their own. Offering some concrete guidance in interpreting nature usually is a good thing, and I am certain that simply
turning students loose within a natural area will fail much of the
time. Nature's lessons are all around, but most people need training to see, hear, and feel them.

An understanding of nature can be compared to language acquisition. At its best, an understanding of nature, like learning a language, comes not with formal lessons and sets of rules, but with
immersion at a time when the mind is most flexible, most open,
and most receptive. Failure to understand nature during this time,
however, does not mean that it cannot be learned at all. It only
means that guidance and formal instruction, along with extended
visits to places where nature is "spoken" may be necessary. This
need for formal training is acknowledged in Taoist thinking. According to Thomas Cleary, "Ancient Taoists considered the harmony of the individual with the universe to be an originally natural
condition, (but) they believed it was already inaccessible to the average person without special means of recovering it."[2]

It is important to state explicitly that understanding nature, in this
instance, means comprehension of the lessons for living that nature offers humanity. It is not environmental science, environmen-

tal politics, environmental philosophy, nor any other kind of environmental studies that traditional education can box up into a structured course. Understanding nature means understanding nature at an intuitive, gut, and/or spiritual level. Classroom-based instruction is important, and I do not want to discount such efforts, but coursework of this type derives most of its value because it stumbles across truths that coincide with students' personal experiences and instinctive knowledge.[3]

## TEACHING NATURE'S LESSONS

To my knowledge, there is no single best way to open people's minds to nature's lessons. I do, however, have four general suggestions for experiential educators who would like to include this goal in their programming. The suggestions all are intended to awaken the aesthetic and contemplative faculties of students.[4] The four are 1) create experiences that make students want to be in nature; 2) help students feel comfortable and safe in wild places; 3) provide lessons that help students rediscover an open and empty mind; 4) and give students examples of the teaching potential of nature.

### SUGGESTION 1: CREATE EXPERIENCES THAT MAKE STUDENTS WANT TO BE IN NATURE. Freeman Tilden wrote that good nature and cultural interpretation is not information, but provocation.[5] By this, he meant that educators should not tell people things, but coax them or entice them to explore a place and learn those things on their own. For example, many years ago I was camping at Acadia National Park in Maine. One evening an interpretative naturalist came to the campground amphitheatre and did a slide show. About half way through the show, there was a beautiful slide of a huge ocean wave colliding with an elaborate rock formation. Immediately several members of the audience asked the naturalist where the rock formation was, and she told us to park in the Sand Beach parking lot and walk south along the shoreline for about a mile. It would be hard to miss. The next morning I went in search of the rock, and I found it. When I found it, however, I also noticed that there was convenient parking only a hundred yards away.

The naturalist had tricked the campground audience (although I prefer to say that she provoked us) into getting out of our cars and exploring a one-mile stretch of shoreline. As a result, the highlight of my short hike was not the rock formation, but the several unplanned experiences that happened along the way. I found a sea cucumber in a tide pool, I snuck up on cormorants when they were underwater and unable to see me, and I photographed a half dozen other rock formations that were nearly as spectacular as the one that I was looking for. A walk that might have taken me 30 minutes took two hours.

Overall, experiential education does a very good job of provoking people into natural areas. To do so is consistent with the basic experiential education tenet of learning by doing. With outdoor recreation as a carrot, experiential educators can use backpacking, canoeing, caving, and rock climbing to draw in people who otherwise would not want to be away from the action of urban life. In many instances, experiential education, especially adventure programming, could do a better job than it does of taking extra time to teach nature appreciation, but conversely, it deserves credit for providing many people with their first introduction to pristine nature.

SUGGESTION 2: HELP STUDENTS TO FEEL COMFORTABLE AND SAFE IN WILD PLACES. In *Nature*, Ralph Waldo Emerson wrote, "Nature always wears the colors of the spirit."[6] Here is something that I, as an experiential educator, can get a hold of. It tells me if I want students to feel warmly toward nature, then I must create a situation where the students are in a positive frame of mind. This means, first of all, that I must make students physically comfortable when they visit nature. If I take students on an outdoor excursion, I have a responsibility to make sure that they remain warm and dry, that the food is plentiful and reasonably good, and that the itinerary is not too demanding for the ability level of the group. If the students are happy and comfortable, their upbeat spirits will see nature as beautiful. If the students are miserable, then nature will take on the color of their discontent. Dewey wrote that one of the primary responsibilities of experiential education is to open doors to new experiences.[7] Nothing closes the door to nature more quickly than a bad first experience. Giving students a bad first experience is not education; it is miseducation. The result of a poorly led outdoor adventure is that the students who never spent time in nature, but were open to the possibility, now realize that wild nature is a miserable place to be. The door that was once ajar, is now closed and locked.

In addition to making students comfortable in nature, experiential education must also make them feel safe in nature. In the story that opened this chapter, the Leader Who is Hardly Known mentioned that some people identify owls with the dangers of the night. One role of experiential education is to break down fears about the natural world. For example, if an experiential educator leads night hikes, those hikes should be laced with stargazing, storytelling, and lessons for "seeing" in the dark. For many people, nature at night means dangerous animals, boogiemen, and a great chance to get lost. It is the job of experiential education to separate the reasonable fears from the irrational ones, address the reasonable ones, help students overcome the irrational ones – and do all this with the goal of making wild nature the welcoming place that many experiential educators know it to be.

SUGGESTION 3: PROVIDE LESSONS TO HELP STUDENTS REDISCOVER AN OPEN AND EMPTY MIND. This suggestion for teaching the lessons of nature was covered extensively in Chapter 11, "The Interrupted Stargazers." Therefore it will not be discussed here, except to say that if experiential educators want to conduct activities that will help to open and empty the mind, I recommend that they look back to the section of The Interrupted Stargazers that talks about quiet watching and walking meditation.

SUGGESTION 4: GIVE STUDENTS EXAMPLES OF THE TEACHING POTENTIAL OF NATURE. There is no master list of nature's wisdom for humankind. In the same way that the Taoist writers cannot rattle off a half dozen hard and fast rules for living right, neither can they, nor can anyone else, say exactly what it is that nature has to teach. Instead, the best that can be done is for an educator to provide examples that are appropriate for a particular time and place. My recommendation is for each experiential educator to slowly compile a series of stories and metaphors that give human meaning to the natural world — and to use them as a learning tool when appropriate. These stories might come from nature writings, from personal experience, or from stories told by others. Cornell[8] and others have published compilations of short nature writings for exactly that purpose, but these generic collections are only a start. The long-term goal should be to have a collection that is site specific and personal. Let me give one example.

Several springs ago I took a group of students canoeing into the backwaters of the Mississippi River near my home in La Crosse, Wisconsin. Because of high water, most of the muskrats dens and beaver lodges were flooded out, and their inhabitants were forced to sleep on top of their homes, instead of inside them. All of the students who were with me on the afternoon paddle saw over two dozen sleeping muskrats in a couple hours on the water. It made for an excellent day of wildlife viewing, but at the time I made no more of it than that. A year later, however, I came across the following passage in *Walden*:

> *The life in us is like the water in the river. It may rise this year higher than man has ever known it, and flood the parched uplands; even this may be the eventful year, which will drown out all our muskrats.... The sun is but a morning star.*[9]

On my own, I would never have equated floods with living life to its fullest, but I was drawn to the image of "drown(ing) out all our muskrats." Am I less with the Tao or less close with nature because the metaphor came from the writings of Thoreau rather than from my own open mind? I do not think so. I feel that I have gained one very good lesson of nature. Furthermore, I like that it was the collaboration of canoe paddling and the reading of Thoreau that generated the metaphor. Independently, neither the trip nor the quotation would have left a lasting impact on me, but together I feel closer to both the river and to the words in *Walden*.

After I discovered Thoreau's muskrat passage, I could not go back and read it to the students who were with me on the afternoon canoe trip. That teaching moment had passed. Now, however, I am ready for the next time. If I encounter flooded out muskrats again, the students with me will get a lesson on living life to its fullest.

This muskrat incident is an example of one of the two kinds of experiences with nature from which to glean meaning. It is as the quiet observer. This is when an event of nature takes place independent of human activity, and a person is fortunate enough to be there to see it with an open mind. The second kind of experience is when a person's presence is key to the event. Climbing a mountain or taking the first step of a thousand-mile journey[10] are obvious examples, although I am more intrigued by the unique, unanticipated, even synchronistic examples that occur to people when they spend a lot of time in natural settings. "The Owl and the Lady's Slipper" is an example of this. It was a person's failure to observe the owl roosting directly in her face that made the experience important. There would have been no lesson had the woman been sitting in the field and simply seen the owl fly to its roost.

Chuangtze wrote that, while imperfect, metaphors are one way to approximate in words that which cannot be expressed in words. Even when words are inadequate, they still may be the best available way to introduce the unexplainable. In fact, Chapter 26 of the *Chuang-tze* offers a nature-based metaphor to explain that if the metaphor takes hold, an understanding of the lesson follows:

> *The fish trap exists because of the fish; once you've gotten the fish, you can forget the trap. The rabbit snare exists because of the rabbit; once you've gotten the rabbit, you can forget the snare. Words exist because of meaning; once you've gotten the meaning, you can forget the words. Where can I find a man who has forgotten the words so that I can have a word with him?*[11]

Tao writings are filled with metaphoric lessons of both the quiet observer and the-presence-of-the-person-is-key types. In *Awakening the Tao*, for example, Lui I-ming uses over 75 metaphors to describe the Tao, and more than half of them are either observations of nature or observations of humankind interacting with nature. For example, in "Thunder and Wind," he wrote, "Thunder is fierce, intense, and strong; wind is gradual, far-reaching, and soft. When wind and thunder combine, then there is soft gentleness in the midst of hard intensity, and there is hard intensity in the midst of gentle softness. Hardness and softness complement each other. What I realize when I observe this is the Tao of balanced harmonization of hardness and softness."[12]

In "Climbing a Mountain, Crossing a River," he wrote, "When you climb a mountain, you put forth effort with every step, not resting until you reach the summit. When you cross a river you take care with every step, not relaxing your attention until you reach the other shore. Even if you have climbed a mountain nearly to the summit, if you leave off that last step to rest your feet, you are still on the way, not yet there. Even if you have crossed a river nearly to the other shore, if you take a careless step, there is still danger. What I realize as I observe this is the Tao of physical effort to carry out the Way."[13]

## CONCLUSION

Compiling lessons of nature is a long-term task. Experiential educators can begin with the universal stories readily available in collected readings, but the real goal is to collect lessons that are personal and site specific. This is not difficult, but it requires patience and an empty mind. Experiencing a place, hearing the stories of others, and reading nature writing will slowly allow nature to reveal her lessons. It is then the role of the experiential educator to receive the message and translate it into a teaching tool for others. As Roger Ames, in "Taoism and the Nature of Nature" described it, "We cannot play the theoretician and derive an environmental ethic by appeal to universal principles, but must apply ourselves to the aesthetic task of cultivating an environmental ethos in our own place and time, and recommending this project to others by our participation in their environments."[14]

The effort, I believe, will be worthwhile. Very possibly there should have been a fifth suggestion to go with the four just described. It would read, "Suggestion 5: Trust that, with training and opportunity, students will openly observe nature on their own." After an experiential educator has brought a student comfortably and safely to nature, has given that student the tools to see nature with an open mind, and has shown that student the potential of nature with a couple of examples, the educator has little choice but to have faith that the efforts will contribute to future experiences in the natural world.

According to Thoreau, the best that teachers can do is open the door to nature as widely as possible and let students walk on through. In *Walden*, he talks about the value of hunting in a way that is very much like Chuang-tze's fish-trap/rabbit snare metaphor. When asked whether children should be taught to hunt, he stated that it is an important part of education because:

> *(a child) is no more humane, while his education has been sadly neglected.... If he goes thither at first as a hunter and fisher, until at last, if he had the seeds of a better life in him, he distinguishes his proper objects, as a poet or naturalist it may be, and leaves the gun and fish-pole behind.*[15]

# SECTION FOUR
## Conclusion

明
師

mentor

I would be a little disappointed if someone
read *The Leader Who is Hardly Known* and con-
cluded that the Tao had nothing new to offer
the field of experiential education. The intent
of the book was to show that the two were kin-
dred perspectives, not that all the best parts of
Tao thinking were already elements of experiential education. My hope was that, in reading
*The Leader Who is Hardly Known*, experiential educators would develop a "trust" in the Tao and be interested in even those Tao concepts that were not part of the experiential education vernacular.

The final chapter of this book, titled "A Town Like Any Other," has
two primary purposes. The first is to remind experiential educators to be open-minded enough to learn from most ideas that
pass their way. If an ancient Chinese philosophy has insights for
contemporary Western-based experiential education, then so too
may other philosophies, theories, and ideas. The second purpose
of the final chapter is to encourage readers to put Tao thinking
into practice. If an experiential educator has stayed with this book
through twelve chapters, there must have been one or two concepts that seemed unique and worthwhile. And if there was something worthwhile, then I think that it is fair to expect a person to
initiate at least one concrete change in their leadership or programming. Such a change might be very small, noticeable to no
one except the person taking the action. The point is to do something. Thoreau left Walden Pond because he needed to get away
from the beaten paths that he had created for himself.[1] Chapter 13
is not asking readers to mirror Thoreau and pick up stakes altogether. It is suggesting that they make small changes for themselves so that experiential education's own beaten paths do not
keep all of us from losing the Way.

MENTOR

# 13

# A Town Like Any Other

Dan, Buzz, and Jen sat at the head of the conference table. They were university students who, for an independent study, had conducted a needs assessment about youth at risk in the small city of Insular. The three had spent the previous two months interviewing the community's teenagers, civic leaders, teachers and counselors, social workers, and business people and were now presenting their interpretation of those interviews to the city's social service committee. The Leader Who is Hardly Known had advised the students on their project, and he sat just off to the side.

The students used a PowerPoint presentation to summarize a series of observations and recommendations, most of which centered on Insular's lack of recreation opportunities for children and adolescents. While a slight oversimplification of the students' conclusions, they basically were saying that much of the vandalism, petty crime, and above all, underage drinking, was in part a result of no organized, socially acceptable alternatives. In other words, the teenagers in Insular had nothing to do.

The three university students were noticeably anxious at the beginning of the presentation, but by the time the meeting had progressed to the question and answer period, they had calmed down and were handling themselves well. Still they were unnerved when one of the committee members said, "I don't want to criticize your effort, because I recognize the serious work that you have done, but how are your recommendations unique to us? Is there anything that you've said today that could not be said of every small city in America?"

After several seconds of uncomfortable silence, the Leader Who is Hardly Known stepped in. "If I may speak for the group," he said, "I think that there are a few things that make Insular unique. First of all, there is an unusually sharp disparity between the services for joiners and those who do not join things. For children and teenagers interested in music or organized sports, your programs are exceptionally good, among the best in the region. Then, however, there is a sharp drop off. If a child or teen is not interested in dedicating four or five afternoons a week to something like orchestra or hockey, there is very little for them to do. Secondly, Insular does not have some of the recreation opportunities that a town of this size usually has; things like a movie theater, a youth center, roller rink, open gyms, or lighted basketball courts. Many people in town actually discourage such facilities for fear that teenagers congregating in one area will lead to delinquent behavior.

"I am not surprised, however, that you find the results of the study ordinary. You know your town much better than any of us, and the things that we found revealing might be common knowledge to you. It is possible that our report is only a confirmation of what you already know, but sometimes a fresh perspective on an old problem is useful."

After the Leader Who is Hardly Known finished his comment, the three students answered a few more questions from the committee, and the meeting ended. The presenters had a forty-mile drive back to the university, and they were barely out of the parking lot when Dan said to the Leader Who is Hardly Known, "Thank you for bailing us out on that one question. I, for one, had no idea what to say."

"Me either," said Jen, "I've never seen a town with so little for kids to do, but when that guy said that Insular was like everyplace else, I realized that I didn't really have much to compare it with. To be honest, he had me wondering whether we had just wasted the last two months on this project."

"Not me," said Buzz. "I didn't answer the question when the man asked it, but it wasn't because I didn't have an answer for him. I was afraid that I was going to tell the guy that he was nuts. His whole town is screwed up, and he doesn't even know it. I come from a town the same size as Insular, and we don't have a third of the problems they have. If the adults in Insular think that their town is normal, their kids don't have a chance. Jen's right. We did just waste the last two months, but not because our results are junk. It's because nobody is going to take our report seriously."

The Leader Who is Hardly Known, listening as he drove down the highway, spoke. "I would not be so quick to discount the value of your work," he said, "but remember it is only a report. Reports are useful when a decision to act has been made, but they are not much for getting people to act in the first place. If and when someone decides to do something about youth-related problems in Insular, they would be foolish not to use your recommendations as a starting point.

"When you originally asked me to advise this project, I agreed to do it not because I thought it would change things in Insular, but because I thought it was a good project for you. Now that you have finished the work, what about it was worthwhile?"

"Oh, this was a good project," said Dan. "Just talking to the teenagers was great. They were kind of jerky, but they were the most honest people we interviewed. All the adults were distrustful. The teachers didn't trust the city officials, and the city officials didn't want to offend anybody. Everybody was quick to blame someone else for the problem, so they couldn't get together to get anything done."

"For me," said Buzz, "the project was represented by the guy who asked the question this morning. Everybody we talked to thought that there was a problem, even a big problem, but almost no one thought that the problem was worse than anyplace else. Actually the only person who thought that Insular was worse off than other towns was the drug and alcohol counselor, and that was because he'd only been living there a year and a half."

"Those are good observations about what might be problems in Insular," said the Leader Who is Hardly Known, "but that is not exactly what I meant to ask. I want you to translate the project into something that can be useful to you."

"I think that it is a perspective thing," said Jen. "I had a romantic notion about small towns. Still do, I guess. Neighbors helping neighbors, people saying hi to strangers when they pass them on the street, that kind of stuff. But with our project, I see the downside as well. Insular seems too removed from the rest of the world. Most of the people there can't see the extent of their problems. They care about their town, but they ignore the things that should be fixed about it."

"Very good point," said the Leader Who is Hardly Known. "You are describing what might be called the dilemma of community. Communities are wonderful things. All of us gain from a sense of community. Communities, however, by definition segregate people from each other. There always are people who are part of the community and people who are not part of the community. Communities are intentionally kept small for the very reasons that Jen thinks small towns are romantic. Yet by staying small, there can be an inbreeding of ideas and a skepticism that the outside can offer anything of value to their unique situation. Communities unconsciously have blind spots. When presented with something new, the results of your study being a good example, a community might welcome it as a breath of fresh air – but it might also discount it as a restatement of what they already know or, worse, as something that does not apply to them, even when it does. The ideal situation, which probably is impossible to achieve, is to have the compassion and cooperative spirit of a healthy community, but not have this spirit lead to a sense that there is little to learn from venturing out."

明
師 TOWARD A TAO LEADERSHIP

*I have long been advocating the teaching of Chinese in sec-
ondary schools, not only because we must inevitably learn
how to communicate with the Chinese themselves, but because, of all the high cultures, theirs is most different from
ours in its ways of thinking. Every culture is based on assumptions so taken for granted that they are barely conscious, and
it is only when we study highly different cultures and languages that we become aware of them.*[1]

Alan Watts

*The Leader Who is Hardly Known* was not written for educators who
are one with the Tao. It was not even written for educators who
aspire to be one with the Tao. The goal was much more modest.
*The Leader Who is Hardly Known* was written for those who are cu-
rious about the Tao or have dabbled in it, but are not sure how to
take this curiosity further. More than anything, the book was written for educators who are open enough to consider Tao thinking
as an educational philosophy and may want to integrate their understanding of the Tao into their professional philosophy and
methodology.

To this end, the final chapter offers two suggestions for putting
Tao thinking into educational practice. They are only suggestions,
intended more as examples than as specific actions to be taken.
My real hope is that the central chapters of the book already have
helped educators come up with their own ideas for action, and
these concluding remarks might spur a couple more. The first suggestion is fairly simple. It is for experiential educators to make no
major changes, but to add small Tao-like elements to their teaching. Such additions might be subtle, but could be the start of a
long journey toward a teaching style laced with Tao elements. The
key to this first suggestion is a commitment to do at least something. It is easy to have good intentions, but fail to act. It is
equally easy to be intimidated by the big task and therefore never

get started. If a Tao-like approach to education makes sense, then a reasonable approach to becoming the Leader Who is Hardly Known is to gently and lightheartedly incorporate the Tao into both programming and leadership style. The journey of a thousand miles, after all, begins with the first step.

The second suggestion is broader than the first, but even it does not call for wholesale revisions. It is merely a Tao twist to an assumption that an effective teacher is, first and foremost, a role model and mentor. The twist is that the role model be a person who is publicly progressing toward the Tao. Whereas the first suggestion is to sprinkle small Tao elements into the education programming, this second suggestion is to put a Tao umbrella over the whole thing. Elaboration of the two suggestions are as follows:

## ADD ONE TAO ELEMENT TO A PROGRAM AND THEN ANOTHER AND THEN ANOTHER

There might come a time when an educator finds teaching according to the Tao effortless and instinctive, but until that occurs, it makes sense to move toward the Tao by taking small, consciously constructed steps. For each educator, the specifics of these steps will vary, differing with site, program, and inclination of that educator. If someone was very excited about incorporating the Tao, I can imagine him or her sitting at a desk, dissecting a program with pen and paper and trying to figure out where Tao thinking might fit in. While I would never discourage anyone with enthusiasm from acting when others are complacent, I do want to mention a less proactive method for incorporating the Tao into experiential education. Rather than brainstorming for ideas, a second method is to wait for Tao elements to reveal themselves. As educators develop an understanding of the Tao, they will begin to recognize the Tao in their current programs. Often these Tao-like moments are one-time, unplanned events, but if an educator notices and earmarks them as worthwhile learning opportunities, they can be developed and made part of the regular programming (or, for that matter, part of the educator's everyday life). Let me give you an example of what I mean.

Maybe because of my background in environmental education, the Tao concepts relating to humankind's relation with nature are especially interesting to me. In particular, I want to be more open-minded when I visit natural areas, and I want my students to be the same. However instead of inventing objectives that will encourage openness, I let my time in nature show me what those objectives ought to be. To date I have compiled only three personal rules-of-thumb, but they are small actions that feel very right for me, and I can adhere to them on a consistent basis. The three are:

OBJECTIVE 1. CONSCIOUSLY REMIND MYSELF TO BE OPEN-MINDED EACH TIME I BEGIN TO HIKE OR CANOE.

The owl pellet story in Chapter 12 is based on a true event. I was the person who was so intent on finding owl pellets that I failed to see an owl that was less than two feet from my face. After that startling occurrence, I began to notice that I often was having companions point out things that I should have noticed on my own. These were not cases of two sets of eyes being better than one; they were examples of me seeing one thing and being blind to another. While fishing from my canoe, I would fail to see a large heron rookery in a nearby stand of trees. While birdwatching, I would notice, but not stop to appreciate the beauty of woodland flowers. I like that my outdoor hobbies motivate me to spend time in nature, just as I am pleased that I can lose myself in my recreation pursuits. Still I realize that I sometimes become so intent on these pursuits that I miss things that I would like to notice and appreciate. Early Twentieth Century Taoist Loy Ching-yuen wrote that focused learning does contribute to an understanding of the Tao, but until a person learns to experience with an open and empty mind, "the desired linking up of heaven and heart can be made more difficult."[2] So, to counterbalance my tendency to over-focus when caught up in outdoor recreation, I deliberately tell myself to be open-minded each time I step onto the trail or into the canoe. I do it by reciting a very short quote from the Huainanzi, which states "People chasing game do not see the mountains."[3]*

---

* I especially like this quote because it counters an Aldo Leopold quote that has long bothered me. Leopold lists the different ways that hunters watch nature, then concludes that "the non-hunter does not watch." Aldo Leopold, *A Sand County Almanac* (New York: Sierra Club/Ballantine, 1966), 224.

OBJECTIVE 2. POLITELY REFUSE TO ANSWER STUDENT QUESTIONS ABOUT GRADES, TESTS, DUE DATES, ETC... WHEN ON A TRAIL OR RIVER. One of the secondary benefits of taking students into nature is that it is a chance for casual one-on-one conversations between student and teacher. On some of my day trips with students in a college-level course, however, these interactions turned into students asking me about class assignments and grading procedures. At first I thought nothing of it, and I answered their questions about the logistics of the course. When it occurred to me that answering such questions was wasting an opportunity to link students to their natural surroundings, I set a class policy that nothing about the mechanics of the course were to be discussed while we were in the outdoors. Even though some students have trouble enjoying nature until their grade-related questions get answered, I ask them to save those questions for the classroom.

OBJECTIVE 3. DURING SOLO HIKES, GENTLY CHANGE MY TRAIN OF THOUGHT WHEN I FIND MYSELF THINKING ABOUT THINGS OF THE CITY.
When I taught environmental education in California, the climax destination of one of my organized hikes was a long-abandoned apple orchard. In the center of the orchard was a large maple with low-hanging branches, so my teenage students each picked a couple green apples and then joined me in the lower branches of the maple. There I read passages from Thoreau's "Walking" and "Wild Apples," while students ate their sour fruit. One of the quotes fit the experience perfectly, because Thoreau wrote about apples too tart for city eating being spicy treats when consumed in the wild.[4] A second Thoreau quote instructed us to enter the forest in spirit, as well as in body,[5] and to that end I had the students leave the orchard one by one and conclude the outing with a solo walk back to camp. While I no longer teach at that environmental education center, the notion of entering the forest in spirit has stayed with me. Therefore when I walk alone on a trail I try to practice a simple walking meditation technique. There is nothing complicated about this; it is just that when I am in a natural area by myself and realize that I am thinking about work, money, or some other non-nature topic, I gently shift my thoughts to the

rhythm of my footsteps. It is easy, and it helps me to have an emptier and more open mind than I would otherwise. Although I use this objective in my personal outings and not my teaching, I think that it has helped me to be a better role model when taking groups into nature.

Obviously these objectives are only examples. They come out of my past experiences, and after trying each a few times, I know they fit with my personality and my teaching responsibilities. All experiential educators can easily develop for themselves similar action lists. The correct approach, I think, is to address the task in a wu wei fashion. A series of easy-to-accomplish objectives that will be carried out over the long-term may be more effective than grandiose changes that cannot be maintained because they demand too much.

## BE THE LEADER WHO IS HARDLY KNOWN

In addition to including incremental Tao-like elements to educational programs, experiential educators who appreciate the Tao can take a broader approach by serving as a Tao-like role model. This means exhibiting attributes consistent with the Tao. Such attributes (e.g., humility, steadiness) have been described in various chapters of this book and do not need elaboration now. Worth mentioning, however, is what it means to be a role model. There is, after all, a bit of paradox here; teaching according to the Tao includes both being a positive role model and being a leader who tends to fade into the background. How, in other words, does a person serve as a role model when his or her educational philosophy is to be noticed as little as necessary?

The answer, I think, is that educators who personify humility, steadiness, and other Tao-like traits will be unusual enough that they, whether they want it or not, will seem out of the ordinary and therefore get noticed by at least the observant students. In a field where many educators are leading with a gung ho enthusiasm, a leader who is hardly known will seem to be a person who "hears a different drummer."[6] To be a role model in accordance with the Tao, there is no need to namedrop terms such as wu-wei or the yin and the yang. There is no need to dress oddly or wear the Tao on one's sleeve. The Tao-like role model is not different to be different, nor Tao-like to be Tao-like. Instead he or she is tranquil, genuine, humble, flexible, and open-minded.[7] As a result, he or she is both different and Tao-like.

There is a Chinese word that I probably should have defined earlier in the book, but I intentionally saved it as a closing. The word is te. Pronounced de (with a short e sound), it has appeared dozens of times in this book as the overlooked second character of the term Tao Te Ching. Tao Te Ching literally means the Classic Book of Tao and Te. Te usually is interpreted as virtue, sometimes as power. Te really means the embodiment of the Tao.[8] Whereas Tao is everywhere, part of the cosmos and part of nature, te is the character of a person who understands and tries to live the Tao. The Shambhala Dictionary of Taoism defines te as the "nature each thing receives from the Tao.... In addition te signifies the virtue attained by realizing the Tao."[9] In other words, by embracing the Tao, a person achieves a virtuous way of living. I am tempted to describe te as a "right way to live," except that Tao would not put it in terms of right or wrong. Te is a matter of finding or losing the Way.

Conscientious teachers can and should ask themselves whether they are being modest, whether they are being genuine, whether they are being flexible, and so on. They can then take all of these admirable traits and place them under the tiny, all-encompassing word that considers all of the Tao; the word te. After I have used over 50,000 words to describe what it is to be a Tao-like educator, here it is in only three; teach with te.

Most experiential educators will never be one with the Tao. Many might come to appreciate the Tao, maybe even love it. That is enough. An effective educator who wishes to teach in accordance with the Tao need not master the Tao to teach with te. He or she can simply be The Leader Who is Hardly Known.

# Noʈes

## Introduction

¹ Lao Tzu, *Tao Te Ching: The Definitive Edition*, trans. Jonathan Star (New York: Jeremy P. Tarcher/Putnam, 2001), 77 (Chapter 64).

² Lao Tzu, *Tao Te Ching*, trans. Ursula K. Le Guin (Boston: Shambhala, 1998), 24 (Chapter 17).

³ Christian Itin, "Reasserting the Philosophy of Experiential Education as a Vehicle for Change in the 21ˢᵗ Century," *Journal of Experiential Education*, Vol. 22(2), 1999, 94.

⁴ Kenneth Boulding, *The Image* (Ann Arbor, MI: University of Michigan Press, 1961), 18.

⁵ Alan W. Watts, *The Way of Zen* (New York: Vintage Books, 1957), 10.

⁶ Alan W. Watts, with collaboration with Al Chung-liang Huang, *Tao: The Watercourse Way* (New York: Pantheon, 1975), 41.

⁷ Lin Yutang, in Laotse, *Wisdom of Laotse*, trans. and ed. Lin Yutang (Westport, CT: Greenwood Press, 1979), 5 .

## Chapter One

¹ The story comes from Chapter 24 of the *Chuangtze*. Translations of the story can be found in Chuang tzu, *The Sayings of Chuang tzu*, trans. James R. Ware (Taipei: Confucius Publishing, 1970); also in Chuang tzu, *The Complete Works of Chuang tzu*, trans. Burton Watson (New York: Columbia University Press, 1968).

² Liu I-ming, *Awakening to the Tao*, trans. Thomas Cleary (Boston: Shambhala, 1988), 48.

³ Lao Tzu, *The Way of Life*, trans. R. B. Blakney (New York: Mentor, 1955), 54 (Chapter 2) .

⁴ Lao Tzu, *Tao Te Ching*, trans. Ursula K. Le Guin (Boston: Shambhala, 1998), 12 (Chapter 9).

⁵ Lao Tzu, *Tao Te Ching*, trans. John C. H. Wu (Boston: Shambhala, 1989), 45 (Chapter 22).

⁶ Lao Tzu, *Tao Te Ching*, trans. Wu, 79 (Chapter 39).

⁷ Lao Tzu, *Tao Te Ching*, trans. Blakney, 120 (Chapter 67).

[8] Plato's Allegory of the Charioteer, for example, says that wisdom must control both the desire for wealth and the desire for fame. In Plato, *Phaedrus*, 253c-257b.

[9] Lin Yutang, *The Importance of Living* (New York: Reynal and Hitchcock, 1937), 102.

[10] Lao Tzu, *Tao Te Ching*, trans. Wu, 35 (Chapter 17).

[11] Chungliang Al Huang and Jerry Lynch, *Mentoring: The Tao of Giving and Receiving Wisdom* (San Francisco: HarperSanFrancisco, 1995), 33.

[12] Liu, *Awakening to the Tao*, 22.

[13] Hua-Ching Ni, *Entering the Tao: Master Ni's Guidance for Self-Cultivation* (Boston: Shambhala, 1997), 50-53.

[14] Thomas Cleary, trans. and ed, *The Spirit of the Tao* (Boston: Shambhala, 1998), 42.

## CHAPTER TWO

[1] This story is my reconstruction of a story from Chapter 30 of the *Chuangtze*. The original story is about swordplay; I changed it to rock climbing. One source of the story is Chuang Tzu, *The Essential Chuang Tzu*, trans. and ed. Sam Hamill and J. P. Seaton (Boston: Shambhala, 1998), 147-151.

[2] Thomas Cleary, trans., *The Book of Leadership and Strategy: Lessons of the Chinese Masters* (Translations from the Taoist Classic Huainanzi). (Boston: Shambala, 1992), 3.

[3] Cleary, *The Book of Leadership and Strategy*, 15.

[4] John Dewey, *Experience and Education* (New York: Simon and Schuster, 1938), 22-23.

[5] Two examples of this perspective are Anne Lindsay and Alan Ewert, "Learning at the Edge: Can Experiential Education Contribute to Educational Reform?" *Journal of Experiential Education*, 22(1), 1999, 12-19; Joel Westheimer, Joseph Kahne, and Amy Gerstein, "School Reform for the Nineties: Opportunities and Obstacles for Experiential Educators," in Richard J. Kraft and James Kielsmeier, eds., *Experiential Learning in Schools and Higher Education* (Dubuque, IA: Kendall/Hunt, 1995), 40-47.

[6] Lao Tzu. *The Complete Works of Lao Tzu: Tao Te Ching and Hua Hu Ching*, trans. Hua-Ching Ni (Santa Monica, CA: Seven Stars Communication, 1979), 119-120.

[7] Chuang Tzu, *Wandering on the Way: Early Taoist Tale and Parables of Chuang Tzu*, trans. Victor H. Mair (Honolulu: University of Hawai'i Press, 1994), 144-145 (Chapter 15) .

[8] Dan Garvey's address is published in Dan Garvey, "We Need Courage: Excerpts from the 1997 Kurt Hahn Address," *Journal of Experiential Education*, Vol. 21(1), 1998, 26-30.

[9] Cleary, *The Book of Leadership and Strategy*, 4,12.

[10] J. Krishnamurti, *Education and the Significance of Life* (San Francisco: HarperSanFrancisco, 1953, 1981), 10.

## CHAPTER THREE

[1] Chungliang Al Huang and Jerry Lynch, *Mentoring: The Tao of Giving and Receiving Wisdom* (San Francisco: HarperSanFrancisco, 1995), 13.

[2] Loren Eiseley, *The Immense Journey* (New York: Vintage Books, 1959), 15.

[3] The watercourse is the primary theme of Alan W. Watts, with collaboration with Al Chung-liang Huang, *Tao: The Watercourse Way* (New York: Pantheon, 1975).

[4] Lao Tzu, *Tao Te Ching*, trans. John C. H. Wu (Boston: Shambhala, 1989), 17, 125, 135, 159 (Chapters 8, 61,66, 78).

[5] Alan W. Watts, *The Way of Zen* (New York: Vintage Books, 1957), 19.

[6] Watts, with collaboration with Huang, *Tao: The Watercourse Way*, 75.

[7] Translator R. B. Blackney actually refers to wu-wei as wei-wu-wei; to act without acting. Lao Tzu, *The Way of Life*, trans. R. B. Blackney (New York: Mentor, 1955), 39.

[8] *Tao Te Ching*, trans. Wu, 35 (Chapter 17).

[9] Gary Snyder, "Buddhism and the Possibilities of a Planetary Culture" in Bill Devall and George Sessions, *Deep Ecology: Living as if Nature Mattered* (Layton, UT: Gibbs M. Smith, 1985), 251-253.

[10] Lin Yutang, *The Importance of Living* (New York: Reynal and Hitchcock, 1937), 161.

[11] *Tao Te Ching*, trans. Wu, 75, 89, 99, 117, 129 (Chapters 37, 43, 48, 57, 63).

[12] Thomas Cleary, trans. and ed., *Wen-tzu: Understanding the Mysteries* (Boston: Shambhala, 1992), 44.

[13] Thomas Cleary, trans. and ed, *The Spirit of the Tao* (Boston: Shambhala, 1998), 92.

[14] Chuang Tzu, *Wandering on the Way: Early Taoist Tale and Parables of Chuang Tzu*, trans. Victor H. Mair (Honolulu: University of Hawai'i Press, 1994), 145 (Chapter 15).

[15] Chuang tzu, *The Complete Works of Chuang tzu*, trans. Burton Watson (New York: Columbia University Press, 1968), 93 (Chapter 7).

[16] Thomas Cleary, trans., *The Essential Tao: An Initiation into the Heart of Taoism through the authentic Tao Te Ching and the Inner Teachings of Chuang Tzu* (San Francisco: HarperSanFrancisco, 1991, 1993), 31 (Chapter 37 of the Tao Te Ching).

[17] At least this is the opinion of Nicky Duenkel and Stephen Streufert, "Do Contrived Adventure Experiences, Such as Ropes Courses, Hinder Participants from Developing a Connection to the Natural World?" In Scott D. Wurdinger and Tom Potter, eds., *Controversial Issues in Adventure Education: A Critical Examination* (Dubuque, IA: Kendall/Hunt, 1999), 195-208.

[18] Kenneth Boulding, *The Image* (Ann Arbor, MI: University of Michigan Press, 1961), 7-9.

[19] John Dewey, *Experience and Education* (New York: Simon and Schuster, 1938),

[20] Watts, with collaboration with Huang, *Tao: The Watercourse Way*, 76.

[21] Huang and Lynch, *Mentoring*, 13.

[22] Thomas Cleary, trans., *The Essential Tao*, 35 (Chapter 43 of the Tao Te Ching).

## CHAPTER FOUR

[1] This argument is made by Kenneth Boulding, *The Image* (Ann Arbor, MI: University of Michigan Press, 1956) 162-163.

[2] Chuang Tzu. 1994. *Wandering on the Way: Early Taoist Tales and Parables of Chuang Tzu*, trans. Victor. H. Mair (Honolulu: University of Hawai'i Press, 1994), 269 (Chapter 26).

[3] Chuang Tzu, *The Essential Chuang Tzu*, trans. and ed. Sam Hamill and J. P. Seaton (Boston: Shambhala, 1998), 4 (Chapter 1).

[4] Thomas Cleary, trans., *The Essential Tao: An Initiation into the Heart of Taoism through the authentic Tao Te Ching and the Inner Teachings of Chuang Tzu* (San Francisco: HarperSanFrancisco, 1991, 1993), 48 (Chapter 63).

[5] Henry David Thoreau, *The Illustrated Walden* (Princeton, NJ: Princeton University Press, 1973) 93.

[6] Chuang Tzu, *The Essential Chuang Tzu*, trans. and ed. Sam Hamill and J. P. Seaton (Boston: Shambhala, 1998), 4 (Chapter 1).

[7] Lao Tzu, *Tao Te Ching*, trans. John C. H. Wu (Boston: Shambhala, 1989), 9 (Chapter 4).

[8] Lin Yutang, *The Importance of Living* (New York: Reynal and Hitchcock, 1937), 162-163.

[9] G. W. Chesterton, *What's Wrong with the World* (New York: Dodd, Mead, 1910), Chapter 14.

[10] John P. Robinson and Geoffrey Godbey, *Time for Life: The Surprising Ways Americans Use Their Time* (University Park, PA: Pennsylvania State University Press, 1997), 39.

[11] Lawrence G. Boldt, *The Tao of Abundance: Eight Ancient Principles for Abundant Living* (New York: Penguin/Arkana, 1999), 203.

[12] Thomas Cleary, trans., *The Book of Leadership and Strategy: Lessons of the Chinese Masters* (Translations from the Taoist Classic Huainanzi). (Boston: Shambala, 1992), 3.

[13] This point is made well by Aldo Leopold, *A Sand County Almanac: With Essays on Conservation from Round River* (New York: Sierra Club/Ballantine Books, 1966), 182-184.

[14] Sebastian deGrazia, *Of Time, Work, and Leisure* (Garden City, NY: Anchor Books, 1964), 13.

[15] Mihalyi Csikszentmihalyi, *The Evolving Self: A Psychology for the Third Millennium* (New York: HarperCollins, 1993), 179-182.

[16] Csikszentmihalyi, *The Evolving Self*, 272-274.

[17] Mark Twain, *Mark Twain Quotations, Newspaper Collections, & Related Resources*, found at http://www.twainquotes.com/Procrastination.html.

[18] James Thurber, "The Shrike and the Chipmunks," in James Thurber, *Fables for our Time and Famous Poems Illustrated*, New York: Harper and Row, 1939, 1940), 22.

[19] Will Rogers, *The Wisdom of Will Rogers*, found at http://www.dobhran.com/greetings/GRinspire178.htm.

[20] W. Somerset Maugham, "The Summing Up," in *Mr. Maugham Himself*, ed. John Beecroft (Garden City, NJ: Doubleday, 1954), 551 (Chapter x).

[21] Thomas Cleary, trans. and ed., *Wen-tzu: Understanding the Mysteries* (Boston: Shambhala, 1992), xiv.

## CHAPTER FIVE

[1] The story appears several places, including Lin Yutang, *The Importance of Living* (New York: Reynal and Hitchcock, 1937), 160; also in Alan Watts, with collaboration with Al Chung-liang Huang, *Tao: The Watercourse Way* (NewYork: Pantheon, 1975), 31.

[2] Thomas Cleary, trans., *The Book of Leadership and Strategy:Lessons of the Chinese Masters (Translations from the Taoist Classic Huainanzi).* (Boston: Shambala, 1992), 95.

[3] Thomas Cleary, trans. and ed, *The Spirit of the Tao* (Boston: Shambhala, 1998), 25.

[4] Lao Tzu, *Tao Te Ching*, trans. John C. H. Wu (Boston: Shambhala, 1989), 67 (Chapter 33).

[5] Cleary, *The Spirit of Tao*, 109.

[6] From "Secret Records of Understanding the Way," in Thomas Cleary, trans., *Taoist Meditation: Methods for Cultivating a Healthy Mind and Body* (Boston: Shambhala, 2000), 127.

[7] Thomas Cleary, trans. and ed., *Wen-tzu: Understanding the Mysteries* (Boston: Shambhala, 1992), 50.

[8] Cleary, *Wen-tzu*, 7.

[9] Cleary, *Wen-tzu*, 10.

[10] Cleary, *Wen-tzu*, 33.

[11] Liu I-ming, *Awakening to the Tao*, trans. Thomas Cleary (Boston: Shambhala, 1988), 70.

[12] Marcus Aurelius, *The Meditations of Marcus Aurelius*, trans. George Long, in *Great Books of the Western World, Vol. 12. Lucretius, Epictetus, Marcus Aurelius.* 1952. (Chicago: Encyclopaedia Britannica, 1952), 273 (Meditation V, No. 34).

[13] Cleary, *The Book of Leadership and Strategy*, 78,87.

[14] Lin Yutang, ed., *The Wisdom of China and India* (New York: Modern Library, 1942), 627.

[15] Chungliang Al Huang and Jerry Lynch, *Mentoring: The Tao of Giving and Receiving Wisdom* (San Francisco: HarperSanFrancisco, 1995), 151.

[16] Lin, *The Importance of Living*, 161.

[17] Eva Wong, trans., *Lieh-tzu: A Taoist Guide to Practical Living* (Boston: Shambhala, 1995), 64.

[18] Alfie Kohn, *No Contest: The Case Against Competition*, Revised Edition (Boston: Houghton Mifflin, 1992), 53-54.

<sup>19</sup> This was anthropology professor Harvey Sarles at the University of Minnesota. I was a Ph.D. student and teaching assistant in the mid 1980's, and one day in one of his classes I complained to the class about a terrible day in an undergraduate course that I was teaching. Sarles responded with this quote.

## Section Two: Teaching Tips

[1] The citations for these three books are Greta K. Nagel, *The Tao of Teaching: The Special Meaning of the Tao Te Ching as Related to the Art and Pleasure of Teaching* (New York: Donald I. Fine , 1999); Pamela K. Metz, *The Tao of Learning* (Atlanta, GA: Humanics, 1998); Patrick Christie, *Teaching in the Tao* (Tucson, AZ: Zephyr Press, 2001).

## Chapter Six

[1] This statement is a paraphrase of two quotes. Chuangtze stated, "When people are pressed too far, they will inevitably respond with evil intentions, not even knowing why they do so." Huainanzi said the same thing by noting that, "When birds are at their wit's end, they peck; when beasts are at their wit's end, they gore; and when humans are at their wit's end, they resort to trickery." Chuang Tzu, *Wandering on the Way: Early Taoist Tale and Parables of Chuang Tzu*, trans. Victor H. Mair (Honolulu: University of Hawai'i Press, 1994), 35 (Chapter 4); also Thomas Cleary, trans., *The Book of Leadership and Strategy: Lessons of the Chinese Masters (Translations from the Taoist Classic Huainanzi)*. (Boston: Shambala, 1992), 9.

[2] Thomas Merton, *A Thomas Merton Reader, Revised Edition*, ed. Thomas B. McDonnell (Garden City, NY: Image Books, 1974), 297.

[3] Chungliang Al Huang and Jerry Lynch, *Mentoring: The Tao of Giving and Receiving Wisdom* (San Francisco: HarperSanFrancisco, 1995), 16.

[4] John L. Luckner and Reldan S. Nadler, *Processing the Experience: Strategies to Enhance and Generalize Learning*, 2d Ed. (Dubuque, IA: Kendall/Hunt, 1997), 28-30.

[5] An example is Chuang Tzu, *Wandering on the Way*, 35.

[6] Laura Joplin, "On Defining Experiential Education," *Journal of Experiential Education*, Spring 1981; Luckner and Nadler, *Processing the Experience*, 258; Simon Priest and Michael A. Gass, *Effective Leadership in Adventure Programming* (Champaign, IL: Human Kinetics, 1997), 21.

[7] Cleary, *The Book of Leadership and Strategy*, 24.

[8] The archetypes of the adventurer and the wanderer come from Carol Pearson's *The Hero Within*. She uses the term warrior rather than adventurer, but I thought adventurer captured better the spirit of conquering the mountain. Carol S. Pearson, *The Hero Within: Six Archetypes We Live By, Expanded Edition* (San Francisco: Harper and Row, 1989).

[9] J. Krishnamurti, *Education and the Significance of Life* (San Francisco: HarperSanFrancisco, 1953), 47.

[10] Chuang Tzu, *Wandering on the Way*, 36, 110.

[11] Chuang Tzu, *Complete Works of Chuang Tzu*, trans. Burton Watson (Columbia University Press, New York, 1968), 93 (Chapter 7).

[12] Thomas E. Smith, Christopher C. Roland, Mark D. Havens, and Judith A. Hoyt, *The Theory and Practice of Challenge Education* (Dubuque, IA: Kendall/Hunt, 1992).

[13] Alan Watts, *Taoism Way Beyond Seeking: The Edited Transcripts* (Boston: Charles E. Tuttle, 1997), 82-83.

[14] Watts, Taoism *Way Beyond Seeking*, 83.

[15] Huang and Lynch, *Mentoring*, 6.

[16] Johan Huizinga, *Homo Ludens: A Study of the Play-Element in Culture* (Boston: Beacon Press, 1950), 13.

[17] Luckner and Nadler, *Processing the Experience*, 258.


CHAPTER SEVEN

[1] Chuang Tzu, *Wandering on the Way: Early Taoist Tale and Parables of Chuang Tzu*, trans. Victor H. Mair (Honolulu: University of Hawai'i Press, 1994), 164, (Chapter 17).

[2] Liu I-ming, *Awakening the Tao*, trans. Thomas Cleary (Boston: Shambhala, 1988), 49-50.

[3] Fritjof Capra, *The Turning Point: Science, Society, and the Rising Culture* (Toronto: Bantam Books, 1982), 39.

[4] Alan W. Watts, with collaboration with Al Chung-liang Huang, *Tao: The Watercourse Way* (New York: Pantheon, 1975), 26.

[5] Liu I-ming, *Awakening the Tao*, trans. Thomas Cleary (Boston: Shambhala, 1988), 18.

[6] Hua-Ching Ni, *Entering the Tao: Master Ni's Guidance for Self-Cultivation* (Boston: Shambhala, 1997), 17.

[7] The anonymously authored One Hundred Proverbs have been translated into English by Lin Yutang ed., *The Wisdom of China and India* (New York: Modern Library, 1942), 1093-1101.

[8] Thomas Merton, *No Man is an Island* (San Diego: Harcourt Brace Hovanovich, 1955), 126-128.

[9] Merton, *No Man is an Island*, 124.

[10] Lawrence G. Boldt, *The Tao of Abundance: Eight Ancient Principles for Abundant Living* (New York: Penguin/Arkana, 1999), 55.

[11] Ni, *Entering the Tao*, 15.

[12] Alan Watts, *The Way of Zen* (New York: Vintage Books, 1956), 10-11.

[13] Liu, *Awakening to the Tao*, 19.

[14] Chuang Tzu, *The Essential Chuang Tzu*, trans. and ed. Sam Hamill and J. P. Seaton (Boston: Shambhala, 1998), 83-84, 87 (Chapter 17).

CHAPTER EIGHT

[1] Thomas Cleary, trans., *The Book of Leadership and Strategy: Lessons of the Chinese Masters* (Translations from the Taoist Classic Huainanzi). (Boston: Shambala, 1992), 36.

[2] Lin, Yutang, *The Importance of Living* (New York: Reynal & Hitchkok, 1937), 112.

[3] This phrase is a fairly common euphemism. For one source, there is Lecture 1 of William James, *Pragmatism*, Bruce Kuklick, ed. (Indianapolis: Hackett, 1981), 8.

[4] Chuang Tzu, *Wandering on the Way: Early Taoist Tale and Parables of Chuang Tzu*, trans. Victor H. Mair (Honolulu: University of Hawai'i Press, 1994), 122 (Chapter 13).

[5] Cleary, *The Book of Leadership and Strategy*, 69.

[6] Lao Tzu, *The Guiding Light of Lao Tzu: An New Translation and Commentary on the Tao Te Ching*, trans. Henry Wei (Wheaton, IL: Theosophical Publishing House, 1982), 150.

[7] Lao Tzu, *The Way of Life*, trans. R. B. Blakney (New York: Mentor, 1955), 69 (Chapter 17).

[8] Lao Tzu, *The Way of Life*, 69.

⁹ Sun Tzu, *The Art of War: A New Translation*, trans. and comment. by the Denma Translation Group (Boston: Shambhala, 2001), 70.

¹⁰ Lin, *The Importance of Living*, 422.


CHAPTER NINE

¹ Lin, Yutang, *The Importance of Living* (New York: Reynal & Hitchkok, 1937), 379.

² Thomas Cleary, trans. and ed., *Wen-tzu: Understanding the Mysteries* (Boston: Shambhala, 1992), 40.

³ J. Krishnamurti, *Education and the Significance of Life* (San Francisco: HarperSanFrancisco, 1953, 1981), 22.

⁴ John Dewey, *Experience and Education* (New York: Simon and Schuster, 1938), 27.

⁵ Greta Nagel, *The Tao of Teaching: The Special Meaning of the Tao Te Ching as Related to the Art and Pleasures of Teaching* (New York: Primus/Donald I. Fine, 1994), 55.

⁶ Lin, *The Importance of Living*, 379.

⁷ This argument has been made by several people, including Joel Meier, "Is the Risk Worth Taking?" in Joel F. Meier, Talmage W. Morash, George E. Welton, Eds., *High-Adventure Outdoor Pursuits: Organization and Leadership* 2d ed. (Columbus, OH: Publishing Horizons, 1987), 23-27.

⁸ Actually this is one of the primary lessons in Kenneth E. Boulding, *The Image* (Ann Arbor, MI: University of Michigan Press, 1961).

⁹ Dewey, *Experience and Education*, 20,25.

¹⁰ Thomas Cleary, trans., *The Book of Leadership and Strategy: Lessons of the Chinese Masters* (Translations from the Taoist Classic Huainanzi). (Boston: Shambala, 1992), 53.

¹¹ Cleary, *The Book of Leadership and Strategy*, 85.

¹² Cleary, *The Book of Leadership and Strategy*, 17.

¹³ Cleary, *The Book of Leadership and Strategy*, 20.

¹⁴ Cleary, *The Book of Leadership and Strategy*, 34.

¹⁵ Cleary, *Wen-tzu,* 76-77.

¹⁶ Liu I-ming, *Awakening the Tao*, trans. Thomas Cleary (Boston: Shambhala, 1988), 37-38.

¹⁷ Liu, *Awakening the Tao,* 13.

¹⁸ Cleary, *The Book of Leadership and Strategy*, 39.

[19] Plato, *Republic, in Five Great Dialogues*, trans.B. Jowett (Roslyn, NY: Walter J. Black, 1942), 427 (Chapter VII).

[20] Lin, *The Importance of Living*, 379.

[21] *The Seventh Generation*. December 15, 1999. Available: http://tuscaroras.com/nativenews/V2N12/seventh_generation.htm.

PART THREE: THE ROLE OF NATURE

[1] Alan W. Watts, *Nature, Man, and Woman* (New York: Vintage Books, 1970), 10.

CHAPTER TEN

[1] Alan Watts, *Nature, Man, and Woman* (New York: Vintage Books, 1970), 83.

[2] Alan Watts, with collaboration with Al Chung-liang Huang, *Tao: The Watercourse Way* (New York: Pantheon, 1975), 32.

[3] Chung-ying Cheng, "On the environmental ethics of the Tao and the Ch'i," *Environmental Ethics*, 8, 1986, 354.

[4] Lao Tzu, *Tao Te Ching*, trans. John C.H. Wu (Boston: Shambhala, 1989), 51 (Chapter 25).

[5] Ralph Waldo Emerson, *Nature* (Boston: James Munroe and Company, 1836), 16-18.

[6] A good example of early planned use of metapor is in Stephen Bacon, *The Conscious Use of Metaphor in Outward Bound* (Denver: Colorado Outward Bound School, 1983).

[7] Roger Ames, "Taoism and the nature of nature," *Environmental Ethics*, Vol. 8, 345.

[8] Lin, Yutang, *The Importance of Living* (New York: Reynal & Hitchkok, 1937), 278-279.

CHAPTER ELEVEN

[1] Annie Dillard, *Pilgrim at Tinker Creek* (New York: Bantam Books, 1974), 33.

[2] John C. Hendee, George H. Stankey, and Robert C. Lucas, *Wilderness Management*: Miscellaneous Publication No. 1365

(Washington, DC: Forest Service, U.S. Department of Agriculture, October 1978), 68.

³ The Wilderness Act. PL 88-577, 88th Congress, September 3, 1964.

⁴ Thomas Cleary, trans. and ed., *Wen-tzu: Understanding the Mysteries*, trans. Thomas Cleary (Boston: Shambhala, 1992), 6.

⁵ Alan Watts, *Nature, Man and Woman* (New York: Vintage Books, 1958), 74.

⁶ Hua-Ching Ni, *Entering the Tao: Master Ni's Guidance for Self-Cultivation* (Boston: Shambhala, 1997), 135-139.

⁷ Ni, *Entering the Tao*, 136.

⁸ Lin Yutang, *The Importance of Living* (New York: Reynal & Hitchcock, 1937), 333.

⁹ Lin, *The Importance of Living*, 333-334.

¹⁰ Henry David Thoreau, *The Selected Works of Henry David Thoreau.* (Boston: Houghton Mifflin Company, 1975), 660, 663.

¹¹ Alan Watts, *Taoism Way Beyond Seeking: The Edited Transcripts* (Boston: Charles E. Tuttle, 1997), 27.

CHAPTER TWELVE

¹ Thomas Cleary, trans. *Went-tzu: Understanding the Mysteries* (Boston: Shambhala, 1992), 38.

² Thomas Cleary, trans., *The Book of Leadership and Strategy: Lessons of the Chinese Masters* (Translations from the Taoist Classic Huainanzi). (Boston: Shambala, 1992), x.

³ Henry David Thoreau, *Walden* (Princeton, NJ: Princeton University Press, 1973), 211.

⁴ One of the earliest American calls for education that awakens aesthetics and reflection is from Frederick Law Olmsted, designer of New York's Central Park and protector of Yosemite Valley. His ideas on the subject can be found in Frederick Law Olmsted, "The Yosemite Valley and the Mariposa big trees," *Landscape Architecture*, Vol. 43, 1952, 13-22.

⁵ Freeman Tilden, *Interpreting Our Heritage* 3rd Ed. (Chapel Hill, NC: University of North Carolina Press, 1977), 9.

⁶ Ralph Waldo Emerson, *Nature* (Boston: James Munroe and Company, 1836), 8.

⁷ John Dewey, *Experience and Education* (New York: Simon and Schuster, 1938), 27.

[8] Examples include Joseph Cornell, *Listening to Nature: How to Deepen Your Awareness of Nature* (Nevada City, CA: Dawn Publication, 1995); David Backes, *The Wilderness Companion: Reflections for the Back-Country Traveler* (Minocqua, WI: NorthWord Press, 1992).

[9] Thoreau, H. D. 1973. *Walden.* Princeton: Princeton University Press, pp. 332-333.

[10] Lao Tzu, *Tao Te Ching*, trans. John C. H. Wu (Boston: Shambhala, 1989), 131 (Chapter 64).

[11] Chuang Tzu, *The Complete Works of Chuang Tzu*, trans. Burton Watson (New York: Columbia University Press, 1968), 302 (Chapter 26).

[12] Liu I-ming, *Awakening the Tao*, trans. Thomas Cleary (Boston: Shambhala, 1988), 5.

[13] Liu, *Awakening the Tao*, 61.

[14] Roger Ames, "Taoism and the nature of nature," *Environmental Ethics*, Vol. 8, 1986, 348.

[15] Thoreau, *Walden*, 212-213.

## PART FOUR: CONCLUSION

[1] Henry David Thoreau, *Walden* (New York: Book-of-the-Month Club, 1996), 426.

## CHAPTER THIRTEEN

[1] Alan Watts, with collaboration with Al Chung-liang Huang, *Tao: The Watercourse Way* (NewYork: Pantheon, 1975), 11.

[2] Loy Ching-yuen, *The Supreme Way: Inner Teachings of the Southern Mountain Tao*, trans. Trevor Carolan and Du Liang (Berkeley, CA: North Atlantic Books, 1997), 32.

[3] Thomas Cleary, trans., *The Book of Leadership and Strategy: Lessons of the Chinese Masters* (Translations from the Taoist Classic Huainanzi). (Boston: Shambala, 1992), 104.

[4] Henry David Thoreau, "Wild Apples," in *The Selected Works of Thoreau*, ed. Walter Harding (Boston: Houghton Mifflin, 1975), 725.

[5] Henry David Thoreau, "Walking," in *The Selected Works of Thoreau*, ed. Walter Harding (Boston: Houghton Mifflin, 1975), 662.

[6] Henry David Thoreau, "Walden," in *The Selected Works of Thoreau*, ed. Walter Harding (Boston: Houghton Mifflin, 1975), 460.

[7] Wang Keping, *The Classic of the Dao: A New Investigation* (Beijing: Foreign Languages Press, 1998), 14.

[8] Palmer, M. 1991. *The Elements of Taoism.* New York: Barnes and Noble Books, pp. 39-40.

[9] Wunsche, Werner, trans., *The Shambhala Dictionary of Taoism*, Ingrid Fischer-Schreiber and David O'Neal, eds. (Boston: Shambhala, 1996), p. 181.

# Bibliography

## TAO AND OTHER ASIAN THINKING

Ames, Roger. "Taoism and the nature of nature," *Environmental Ethics*, Vol. 8, 1986, 317-350.

Boldt, Lawrence G. *The Tao of Abundance: Eight Ancient Principles for Abundant Living*. New York: Penguin/Arkana, 1999.

Cheng Chung-ying. "On the environmental ethics of the Tao and the Ch'i," *Environmental Ethics*, 8, 1986, 351-370.

Christie, Patrick. *Teaching in the Tao*. Tucson, AZ: Zephyr Press, 2001.

Chuang Tzu. *The Complete Works of Chuang Tzu*. Trans. Burton Watson. New York: Columbia University Press, 1968.

————. *The Essential Chuang Tzu*. Trans. and Ed. Sam Hamill and J. P. Seaton. Boston: Shambhala, 1998.

————. *The Sayings of Chuang Tzu*. Trans. James R. Ware. Taipei: Confucius Publishing, 1970.

————. *Wandering on the Way: Early Taoist Tales and Parables of Chuang Tzu*. Trans. Victor H. Mair. Honolulu: University of Hawai'i Press, 1994.

Cleary, Thomas, trans., *Taoist Meditation: Methods for Cultivating a Healthy Mind and Body*. Boston: Shambhala, 2000.

————. trans., *The Book of Leadership and Strategy: Lessons of the Chinese Masters (Translations from the Taoist Classic Huainanzi)*. Boston: Shambala, 1992.

————. trans., *The Essential Tao: An Initiation into the Heart of Taoism through the authentic Tao Te Ching and the Inner Teachings of Chuang Tzu*. San Francisco: HarperSanFrancisco, 1991, 1993.

————. trans. and ed., *The Spirit of the Tao*. Boston: Shambhala, 1998.

————. trans. and ed., *Wen-tzu: Understanding the Mysteries*. Boston: Shambhala, 1992.

Snyder, Gary. "Buddhism and the Possibilities of a Planetary Culture" in Bill Devall and George Sessions, *Deep Ecology: Living as if Nature Mattered*. Layton, UT: Gibbs M. Smith, 1985.

Huang, Chungliang Al, and Jerry Lynch. *Mentoring: The Tao of Giving and Receiving Wisdom*. San Francisco: HarperSanFrancisco, 1995.

Krishnamurti, J. *Education and the Significance of Life*. San Francisco: HarperSanFrancisco, 1953.

Lao Tzu. *Tao Te Ching. The Complete Works of Lao Tzu: Tao Te Ching and Hua Hu Ching.* Trans. Hua-Ching Ni. Santa Monica, CA: Seven Stars Communication, 1979.

———. *The Guiding Light of Lao Tzu: An New Translation and Commentary on the Tao Te Ching.* Trans. Henry Wei. Wheaton, IL: Theosophical Publishing House, 1982.

———. *Tao Te Ching.* Trans. John C. H. Wu. Boston: Shambhala, 1989.

———. *Tao Te Ching.* Trans. Ursula K. Le Guin. Boston: Shambhala, 1998.

———. *Tao Te Ching: The Definitive Edition.* Trans. Jonathan Star. New York: Jeremy P. Tarcher/Putnam, 2001.

———. *The Way of Life.* Trans. R. B. Blakney. New York: Mentor, 1955.

Laotse. *Wisdom of Laotse.* Trans. and Ed. Lin Yutang. Westport, CT: Greenwood Press, 1979.

Lin Yutang. *The Importance of Living.* New York: Reynal and Hitchcock, 1937.

———. ed. *The Wisdom of China and India.* New York: Modern Library, 1942.

Liu I-ming. *Awakening the Tao.* Trans. Thomas Cleary. Boston: Shambhala, 1988.

Loy Ching-yuen. *The Supreme Way: Inner Teachings of the Southern Mountain Tao.* Trans. Trevor Carolan and Du Liang. Berkeley, CA: North Atlantic Books, 1997.

Metz, Pamela K. *The Tao of Learning.* Atlanta, GA :Humanics, 1998.

Nagel, Greta K. *The Tao of Teaching: The Special Meaning of the Tao Te Ching as Related to the Art and Pleasure of Teaching.* New York: Primus/Donald I. Fine, 1999.

Ni, Hua-Ching. *Entering the Tao: Master Ni's Guidance for Self-Cultivation.* Boston: Shambhala, 1997.

Palmer, Martin. *The Elements of Taoism.* New York: Barnes and Noble Books, 1991.

Ram Dass. *Journey of Awakening: A Meditator's Handbook,* Revised Edition. New York: Bantam Books, 1990.

Sun Tzu. *The Art of War: A New Translation.* Trans. and Comment by the Denma Translation Group. Boston: Shambhala, 2001.

Wang Keping. *The Classic of the Dao: A New Investigation.* Beijing: Foreign Languages Press, 1998.

Watts, Alan. *Nature, Man, and Woman.* New York: Vintage Books, 1970.

———— with collaboration with Al Chung-liang Huang. *Tao: The Watercourse Way.* New York: Pantheon, 1975.

————. *Taoism Way Beyond Seeking: The Edited Transcripts.* Boston: Charles E. Tuttle, 1997.

————. *The Way of Zen.* New York: Vintage Books, 1957.

Wong, Eva, trans. *Lieh-tzu: A Taoist Guide to Practical Living.* Boston: Shambhala, 1995.

Wunsche, Werner, trans. *The Shambhala Dictionary of Taoism.* Eds. Ingrid Fischer-Schreiber and David O'Neal. Boston: Shambhala, 1996.

## EXPERIENTIAL EDUCATION, ADVENTURE EDUCATION, AND ENVIRONMENTAL EDUCATION

Backes, David. *The Wilderness Companion: Reflections for the Back-Country Traveler.* Minocqua, WI: NorthWord Press, 1992.

Bacon, Stephen. *The Conscious Use of Metaphor in Outward Bound.* Denver: Colorado Outward Bound School, 1983.

Cornell. *Listening to Nature: How to Deepen Your Awareness of Nature.* Nevada City, CA: Dawn Publication, 1995.

Dewey, John. *Experience and Education.* New York: Simon and Schuster, 1938.

Duenkel, Nicky, and Stephen Streufert. "Do Contrived Adventure Experiences, Such as Ropes Courses, Hinder Participants from Developing a Connection to the Natural World?" In Scott D. Wurdinger and Tom Potter, eds., *Controversial Issues in Adventure Education: A Critical Examination.* Dubuque, IA: Kendall/Hunt, 1999.

Garvey, Dan. "We Need Courage: Excerpts from the 1997 Kurt Hahn Address," *Journal of Experiential Education*, Vol. 21(1), 1998, 26-30.

Itin, Christian. "Reasserting the Philosophy of Experiential Education as a Vehicle for Change in the 21st Century." *Journal of Experiential Education*, Vol. 22(2), 1999, 91-98.

Joplin, Laura. "On Defining Experiential Education." *Journal of Experiential Education*, Spring 1981.

Lindsay, Anne, and Alan Ewert. "Learning at the Edge: Can Experiential Education Contribute to Educational Reform?" *Journal of Experiential Education*, 22(1), 1999, 12-19.

Luckner, John L., and Reldan S. Nadler. *Processing the Experience: Strategies to Enhance and Generalize Learning*, 2d Ed. Dubuque, IA: Kendall/Hunt, 1997.

Meier, Joel. "Is the Risk Worth Taking?" in Joel F. Meier, Talmage W. Morash, George E. Welton, Eds., *High-Adventure Outdoor Pursuits: Organization and Leadership* 2d Ed. Columbus, OH: Publishing Horizons, 1987.

Priest, Simon, and Michael A. Gass. *Effective Leadership in Adventure Programming*. Champaign, IL: Human Kinetics, 1997.

Smith, Thomas E., Christopher C. Roland, Mark D. Havens, and Judith A. Hoyt. *The Theory and Practice of Challenge Education* Dubuque, IA: Kendall/Hunt, 1992.

Westheimer, Joel, Joseph Kahne, and Amy Gerstein. "School Reform for the Nineties: Opportunities and Obstacles for Experiential Educators." in Richard J. Kraft and James Kielsmeier, eds., *Experiential Learning in Schools and Higher Education*. Dubuque, IA: Kendall/Hunt, 1995.

WESTERN PHILOSOPHY, NATURE WRITING, AND OTHER RESOURCES

Aristotle. *Ethics*. Trans. J. A. K. Thomson. Middlesex: Penguin, 1976.

Aurelius, Marcus. *The Meditations of Marcus Aurelius*. Trans. George Long, in *Great Books of the Western World, Vol. 12. Lucretius, Epictetus, Marcus Aurelius*. Chicago: Encyclopaedia Britannica, 1952.

Boulding, Kenneth. *The Image*. Ann Arbor, MI: University of Michigan Press, 1961.

Chesterton, G. W. *What's Wrong with the World*. New York: Dodd, Mead, 1910.

Csikszentmihalyi, Mihalyi. *The Evolving Self: A Psychology for the Third Millennium*. New York: HarperCollins, 1993.

deGrazia, Sebastion. *Of Time, Work, and Leisure*. Garden City, NY: Anchor Books, 1964.

Dillard, Annie. *Pilgrim at Tinker Creek.* New York: Bantam Books, 1974.

Eiseley, Loren. *The Immense Journey.* New York: Vintage Books, 1959.

Emerson, Ralph Waldo. *Nature.* Boston: James Munroe and Company, 1836.

Hendee, John C., George H. Stankey, and Robert C. Lucas. *Wilderness Management: Miscellaneous Publication No. 1365.* Washington, DC: Forest Service, U.S. Department of Agriculture, October 1978.

Huizinga, Johan. *Homo Ludens: A Study of the Play-Element in Culture.* Boston: Beacon Press, 1950.

James, William. *Pragmatism.* Ed. Bruce Kuklick. Indianapolis: Hackett, 1981.

Kohn, Alfie. *No Contest: The Case Against Competition,* Revised Edition. Boston: Houghton Mifflin, 1992.

Leopold. *A Sand County Almanac: With Essays on Conservation from Round River.* New York: Sierra Club/Ballantine Books, 1966.

Maugham, W. Somerset. "The Summing Up," in *Mr. Maugham Himself.* Ed. John Beecroft. Garden City, NJ: Doubleday, 1954.

Merton, Thomas. *A Thomas Merton Reader, Revised Edition.* Ed. Thomas B. McDonnell. Garden City, NY: Image Books, 1974.

———. *No Man is an Island.* San Diego: Harcourt Brace Hovanovich, 1955.

Olmsted, Frederick Law. "The Yosemite Valley and the Mariposa big trees," *Landscape Architecture,* Vol. 43, 1952, 13-22.

Pearson, Carol S. *The Hero Within: Six Archetypes We Live By,* Expanded Edition. San Francisco: Harper and Row, 1989.

Pieper, Josef. *Leisure: The Basis of Culture.* Indianapolis, Liberty Fund, 1952.

Plato. *Phaedrus.* 253c-257b.

———. *Republic,* in *Five Great Dialogues.* Trans. B. Jowett. Roslyn, NY: Walter J. Black, 1942.

Robinson, John P., and Geoffrey Godbey. *Time for Life: The Surprising Ways Americans Use Their Time.* University Park, PA: Pennsylvania State University Press, 1997.

Rogers, Will. *The Wisdom of Will Rogers,* found at http://www.dobhran.com/greetings/GRinspire178.htm.

*The Seventh Generation.* December 15, 1999. Available: http://tuscaroras.com/nativenews/V2N12/seventh_generation.htm.

Thoreau, Henry David. *The Selected Works of Henry David Thoreau*. Ed. Walter Harding. Boston: Houghton Mifflin Company, 1975.
———. *Walden*. Princeton, NJ: Princeton University Press, 1973.
Thurber, James. "The Shrike and the Chipmunks," in James Thurber, *Fables for our Time and Famous Poems Illustrated*. New York: Harper and Row, 1939, 1940.
Tilden, Freeman. *Interpreting Our Heritage* 3rd Ed. Chapel Hill, NC: University of North Carolina Press, 1977.
Twain, *Mark Twain Quotations, Newspaper Collections, & Related Resources*, found at http://www.twainquotes.com/ Procrastination.html.
Wilderness Act. PL 88-577, 88th Congress, September 3, 1964.